Lesson Plans
for
Classroom
Teachers

Kindergarten through Second Grade

Robert P. Pangrazi
Arizona State University

Allyn and Bacon
Boston · London · Toronto · Sydney · Tokyo · Singapore

Copyright © 1997 by Allyn & Bacon
A Viacom Company
160 Gould Street
Needham Heights, Massachusetts 02194

Internet: www.abacon.com
America Online: keyword: College Online

ISBN 0-205-19363-3

Printed in the United States of America

10 9 8 7 6 5 4 3 2   01 00 99 98

Library of Congress Cataloging-in-Publication Data

Pangrazi, Robert P.
    Lesson plans for classroom teachers. Kindergarten through second
grade / Robert P. Pangrazi.
        p.   cm.
    ISBN 0-205-19363-3 (pbk.)
    1. Physical education for children. 2. Movement education.
3. Lesson planning. 4. Kindergarten--Curricula. 5. Education,
Primary--Curricula.   I. Title.
GV443.P34434 1996
372.86043--dc21   96-46298
                                                             CIP

13.95   7-20-98

LESSON PLANS FOR THE SCHOOL YEAR
Kindergarten through Second Grade

WEEK	INTRODUCTORY ACTIVITY	FITNESS DEVELOPMENT ACTIVITY	LESSON FOCUS ACTIVITY	GAME ACTIVITY	PAGE
1	Move and Freeze on Signal	Teacher Leader Movement Challenges	Orientation and Class Management Activities	Class Management Games	1
2	Move and Assume Pose	Parachute Fitness	Tossing and Catching Skills	Midnight Leap the Brook	3
3	Locomotor Movements and Freeze	Movement Challenges	Fundamental Skills Using Hoops	Mat Game Sneak Attack	5
4	Hoops - Free Activity	Walk, Trot, and Jog	Kicking, Trapping, Bowling, and Rolling	Back to Back Change Sides Musical Ball Pass	8
5	European Running	Jump Rope Exercises	Movement Skills (1) Walking, Body Part Identification, and Personal Space	Jack Frost and Jane Thaw Marching Ponies Tag Games	10
6	Magic Number Challenges	Animal Movements and Fitness Challenges	Rhythmic Movement(1)	Squirrel in the Trees Stop Ball	13
7	Crossing the River	Circuit Training	Long Rope Jumping Skills	Ball Passing Hot Potatoes Aviator	16
8	Combination Movements	Fitness Challenges	Manipulative Skills Using Playground Balls	Teacher Ball The Scarecrow and the Crows	18
9	Bend, Stretch, and Shake	Fitness Games and Challenges	Movement Skills and Concepts Using Jump Rope Patterns	Tag Games Charlie Over the Water Flowers and Wind	21
10	Marking	Parachute Fitness	Movement Skills(2) Jumping, Tossing & Catching, & Moving in Space	Firefighter Animal Tag Sneak Attack	23
11	Individual Movement with Manipulation	Four Corners Fitness	Individual Rope Jumping Skills	Tommy Tucker's Land Change Sides	26
12	Movement Varieties	Circuit Training	Movement Skills (3) Running and Racquet Skills	Rollee Pollee Mix and Match	28
13	New Leader Warm-Up	Jump Rope Exercises	Rhythmic Movement (2)	Bottle Kick Ball Hill Dill	31
14	Group Over and Under	Astronaut Drills	Throwing Skills(1)	Aviator Sneak Attack	34

Using The Lesson Plans

The lesson plans provide a guide for presenting movement experiences in a sequential and well-ordered manner. The series of plans serve as a comprehensive curriculum. Lessons can be modified and shaped to meet the needs of individual teachers. Many teachers take activities from the lesson plans and write them on 4" by 6" note cards. All lesson presentations should be mentally rehearsed to prevent excessive use of written notes. Lesson plan note cards help relieve the burden of trying to remember the proper sequence of activities and the worry of forgetting key points of instruction.

Grade Levels

Three sets of lesson plans are available to cover the Kindergarten through sixth grade curriculum. The following is a brief description about the content included in each set of lesson plans:

Kindergarten through Second Grade. Learner characteristics of children in grades K-2 dictate the need for an enjoyable and instructional learning environment. By stressing the joy of physical activity, positive behaviors are developed that last a lifetime. The majority of activities for younger children are individual in nature and center on learning movement concepts through theme development. Children learn about basic movement principles and educational movement themes are used to teach body identification and body management skills.

Third Grade through Fourth Grade. Activities for children in this age group focus on refinement of fundamental skills and the introduction of specialized sport skills. Visual-tactile coordination is enhanced by using a variety of manipulative skills. Children should be allowed the opportunity to explore, experiment, and create activities without fear. While not stressing conformity, children need to absorb the how and also the why of activity patterns. Cooperation with peers is important as more emphasis is placed on group and team activities. Initial instruction in sport skills begins at this level and a number of lead-up activities are utilized so youngsters can apply newly learned skills in a small group setting.

Fifth Grade through Sixth Grade. Physical education instruction moves toward specialized skills and sport activities. Football, basketball, softball, track and field, volleyball, and hockey are added to the sport offerings. Students continue learning and improving sport skills while participating in cooperative sport lead-up games. Less emphasis is placed on movement concept activities and a larger percentage of instructional time is devoted to manipulative activity. Adequate time is set aside for the rhythmic program and for the program area involving apparatus, stunts, and tumbling. At this level, increased emphasis is placed on physical fitness and developmental activities. Organized and structured fitness routines are offered so that students can begin to make decisions about personal approaches to maintaining fitness levels.

Format of the Lesson Plans

Each lesson plan is divided into four instructional parts and contains enough activities for a week of instruction. Briefly, the four instructional parts of the lesson plan and major purposes of each section are as follows:

Introductory Activity: Introductory activities change weekly and are used to physiologically prepare children for activity when entering the gymnasium or activity area. Activities used in this section demand little instruction and allow time for practicing class management skills.

Fitness Development Activity: Fitness activities take 7 to 8 minutes of a 30 minute lesson. The activities should be personalized, progressive in nature, and exercise all parts of the body. Allied to the workout should be brief discussions about the values of fitness for a healthy lifestyle. A comprehensive discussion of fitness principles, fitness activities, and instructional guidelines is found in Chapter 8 of the textbook.

Lesson Focus Activities: The purpose of the lesson focus is to teach children major program objectives such as the development of eye-hand coordination, body management competency, and fundamental and specialized skills (e.g., folk dancing, shooting a basket, and catching an object). The lesson focus uses 15-20 minutes of the daily lesson depending on the length of the teaching period. Lesson focus activities are organized into units and vary in length depending on the developmental level of children. Lesson focus activities are changed weekly except when continuity of instruction demands longer units. Enough activities are placed in each lesson focus section to accommodate three to four teaching periods.

The content in each lesson is organized in a developmental sequence, with the first activity being the easiest and the last activity the most difficult. Usually, instruction starts with the first activity and proceeds forward regardless of developmental level. The implications are twofold: This progression ensures that each unit begins with success, since all children are capable of performing the beginning activities. It also assures that a proper sequence of activities will be followed during instruction. Obviously, developmentally mature children will progress further along the continuum of activities than less capable children.

Game Activity: This part of the lesson plan takes place at the closing of the lesson, utilizing the last 5-7 minutes of the period. Games are often used as a culminating activity for practicing skills emphasized in the lesson focus. In other lessons, games are unrelated to the lesson focus and are presented for the purpose of completing the lesson with a fun and enjoyable activity. The game should leave children with positive feelings so they look forward with anticipation to the next lesson. If the lesson has been physically demanding, a less active game can be played and vice versa. In some cases, a low key, relaxing activity might be chosen so that children can unwind before returning to the classroom.

Contents of the Lesson Plans

Objectives and required equipment are listed at the top of each lesson plan. This establishes the reason for teaching the lesson and makes it easy to prepare the equipment for instruction. The contents of the lesson plans is placed into two columns:

Instructional Activities: This column lists activities that will be taught in the lesson. The content in this column offers progression and sequence for activities that will be presented during the week. All activities are explained in detail and can be presented easily from each lesson plan.

Teaching Hints: This section provides points for efficient organization of the class and important learning cues. Emphasis in this column is on teaching for quality of movement rather than quantity.

Lesson Plans for Grades K-2 - Week 1
Orientation and Class Management Activities

Objectives:
To learn and follow basic management activities necessary for participation in
  physical education classes

Equipment Required:
Tom-tom
Tape player and music for fitness
  challenges

Instructional Activities	Teaching Hints

Orientation Instructional Procedures

The first week of school should be used to teach students the system you are going to use throughout the year. The following are reminders you might find useful in establishing your expectations and routines.

1. Establish rules and expectations. Discuss your expectations with the class to assure students understand reasons for your guidelines. Explain what the consequences are when rules are not followed. Show where time-out boxes are located and how they will be used.

2. Explain to the class the method you will use to learn names. It might be helpful to ask classroom teachers to have students put their name on a piece of masking tape (name tag). Tell students that you will ask them their name on a regular basis until it is learned.

3. Develop entry and exit behaviors for students coming and leaving physical education classes. Students should know how to enter the instructional area and to leave equipment alone until told to use it. If squads are used for instruction, place students into squads and practice moving into formation on signal.

4. Decide how excuses for non-participation will be handled. If possible, set up a routine where the school nurse determines which students are excused for health reasons.

5. Safety is important. Children should receive safety rules to be followed on apparatus and playground equipment. Safety procedures to be followed in physical education classes should be discussed.

6. Illustrate how you will stop and start the class. In general, a whistle (or similar loud signal) and a raised hand is effective for stopping the class. A voice command should be used to start the class. Telling the class when before what (Chapter 5) will assure they do not begin before instructions are finished.

7. Discuss the issue, distribution, and care of equipment. Make students responsible for acquiring a piece of equipment and returning it at the end of the lesson. Place equipment around the perimeter of the teaching area to reduce the chance of students fighting over a piece of equipment.

8. Explain to the class that the format of the daily lesson will include an introductory activity, fitness development, lesson focus, and finish with a game activity.

9. Practice various teaching formations such as open-squad formation and closed-squad formation. Practice moving into a circle while moving (fall-in). Transitions between formations should be done while moving, i.e., jogging from scatter formation into a circular formation.

10. Refer to Chapters 4 and 5 in the text for detailed information about planning, developing an effective learning environment, and class management strategies.

Introductory Activity -- Move and Freeze on Signal

Have students move throughout the area using a variety of locomotor movements. On signal (whistle), they quickly freeze. Try to reduce the response latency by reinforcing students who stop quickly on signal.

The primary objective is to teach students the importance of moving under control (without bumping others or falling down) and quickly freezing.

Fitness Development Activity -- Teacher Leader Movement Challenges

1. Locomotor Movement: Walk for 30 seconds.

2. Flexibility and Trunk Development Challenges
    a. Bend in different directions.
    b. Stretch slowly and return quickly.
    c. Combine bending and stretching movements.
    d. Sway back and forth.
    e. Twist one body part; add body parts.

3. Locomotor Movement: Skip for 30 seconds.

4. Shoulder Girdle Challenges
In a push-up position, do the following challenges:
    a. Lift one foot; the other foot.
    b. Wave at a friend; wave with the other arm.
    c. Scratch your back with one hand; use the other hand.
    d. Walk your feet to your hands.

5. Locomotor Movement: Jog for 30 seconds.

6. Abdominal Development Challenges
From a supine position:
    1. Lift your head and look at your toes.
    2. Lift your knees to your chest.
    3. Wave your legs at a friend.
From a sitting position;
    1. Slowly lay down with hands on tummy.
    2. Lift legs and touch toes.

7. Locomotor Movement: Run and leap for 30 seconds.

The goal should be to move students through a number of movement challenges. Emphasis should be placed on starting the fitness activities at a level where all students can feel successful.

Alternate the locomotor movements with the strength and flexibility challenges. Repeat the challenges as necessary.

Tape alternating segments (30 seconds in length) of silence and music to signal duration of exercise. Music segments indicate locomotor movements while intervals of silence announce doing the movement challenges.

Teach youngsters the different challenges and then allow them to select a challenge they can successfully perform.

The challenges should be enjoyable to perform.

See text, p. 163-167 for descriptions of challenges.

Workloads should be moderate with emphasis on success for all youngsters.

Lesson Focus – Orientation

Since much time during the first week is used for orientation procedures and management, no lesson focus activity is scheduled.

Game Activity -- Management Games

Play one or two management games to teach students how to move into partner and small group formation

Back to Back
Supplies: None
Skills: Fundamental locomotor movements
Students move under control throughout the area using a variety of locomotor movements. On signal, each child stands back to back (or toe to toe) with another child. If one child ends up without a partner, the teacher takes this student as a partner. Youngsters who do not find a partner nearby run to a designated spot in the center of the area. This helps assure that students do not run around looking for a partner or feel left out. Students who move to the center spot quickly find a partner and move out of the area (to avoid crowding around the center spot). Emphasis should be placed on finding a partner nearby rather than searching for a friend. Have students find a different partner each time.

Whistle Mixer
Supplies: None
Skills: All basic locomotor movements
Children are scattered throughout the area. To begin, they move in any direction they wish. The teacher whistles a number of times in succession and raises the same number of fingers above their head to signal the group size. Children then form small groups with the number in each group equal to the number of whistles. For example, if there are four short whistles, children form circles of four--no more, no less. The goal is to find the correct number of students as quickly as possible. As soon as a group has the desired number, they sit down to signal that other may not join the group. Children who cannot find a group nearby should move to the center of the area and raise their hands to facilitate finding others without a group.

Lesson Plans for Grades K-2 - Week 2
Tossing and Catching Skills

Objectives:
To move in a large group without bumping into others
To freeze on signal
To learn tossing and catching skills.
To cooperate in game activities

Equipment Required:
One beanbag per student
Parachute
Taped music and player

Instructional Activities	Teaching Hints

Introductory Activity -- Move and Assume Pose

Have children move using a variety of locomotor movements. Freeze on signal and assume a pose. The following position are suggested:
1. Balance on different body parts
2. Stretch
3. Curl
4. Bridge
5. Push-up position
6. V-Sit position
7. Seat Circle
8. Stork Stand

Ask class to start moving upon entry into teaching area.

Freeze means not moving or talking.

Check the variety of poses.

Reinforce stopping without falling.

Fitness Development Activity -- Parachute Fitness

1. Jog while holding the chute in the left hand. (music)
2. Shake the chute. (no music)
3. Slide while holding the chute with both hands. (music)
4. Sit and perform curl-ups - (no music)
5. Skip. (music)
6. Freeze, face the center, and stretch the chute tightly. Hold for 8-12 seconds. Repeat five to six times. (no music)
7. Run in place while holding the chute taut at different levels. (music)
8. Sit with legs under the chute. Do a seat walk toward the center. Return to the perimeter. Repeat four to six times. (no music)
9. Place the chute on the ground. Jog away from the chute and return on signal. Repeat. (music)
10. Move into push-up position holding the chute with one hand. Shake the chute. (no music)
11. Shake the chute and jump in place. (music)
12. Lie on back with feet under the chute. Shake the chute with the feet. (no music)
13. Hop to the center of the chute and return. Repeat. (music)
14. Sit with feet under the chute. Stretch by touching the toes with the chute. Relax with other stretches while sitting. (no music)

Tape alternating segments (20 seconds in length) of silence and music to signal duration of exercise. Music segments indicate aerobic activity with the parachute while intervals of silence announce using the chute to enhance flexibility and strength development.

Space youngsters evenly around the chute.

Use different hand grips (palms up, down, mixed).

All movements should be done under control. Some of the faster and stronger students will have to moderate their performance.

Lesson Focus -- Manipulative Skills with Beanbags

Stand in place and practice tossing and catching
1. Toss and catch with both hands - right hand, left hand
2. Toss and catch with the back of hands. This will encourage children to catch with "soft hands."
3. Toss the beanbag to an increasingly high level, emphasizing a straight overhead toss. To encourage straight tossing, have the child sit down.

Stand in place, toss and catch while performing stunts
1. Toss overhead and perform the following stunts and catch the bag.
   a. ¼ and ½ turns, right and left
   b. Full turn
   c. Touch floor
   d. Clap hands
   e. Clap hands around different parts of body, behind back, under legs.

Each student must have a beanbag for practice.

Give students two or three activities to practice so you have time to move and help individuals. Alternate activities from each of the categories so students receive a variety of skills to practice.

Emphasize tosses that are straight up and about 12 inches above the head.

f. Heel click

g. Sit down, get up

h. Look between legs

Toss, move to a new spot and catch the beanbag

1. Toss overhead, move to another spot, and catch.
2. Toss, do a locomotor movement, and catch.
3. Toss and move from side to side.
4. Toss overhead behind self, move, and catch.

This is an excellent activity for teaching students to track (keep their eyes focused on) the beanbag. Remind them not to look away while tossing and catching.

Balance the beanbag

1. Balance on the following body parts
   a. Head
   b. Back of hand
   c. Shoulder
   d. Knee
   e. Foot
   f. Elbow
   g. Exploratory activity
2. Balance and move as follows:
   a. Walk
   b. Run
   c. Skip
   d. Gallop
   e. Sit down
   f. Lie down
   g. Turn around
   h. Combinations of the above
   i. Exploratory activity

Students should be encouraged to see how long they can balance the beanbag.

Movements should be controlled with as little bounce as possible.

These are body control activities. Students must be able to concentrate on moving slowly and keeping the beanbag in place.

Use the challenge to motivate students. These activities will be exciting and should be integrated throughout the lesson.

Beanbag challenge activities

1. Hold the beanbag between knees and play tag with a partner or small group.
2. Place the beanbag on tummy and shake it off.
3. Place the beanbag on back and Mule Kick it off.
4. Push the beanbag across the floor with different body parts.
5. Toss the beanbag up and touch specified body parts.
6. Put beanbags on floor. Rotate various body parts on a beanbag.
7. Beanbag Balance Tag - balance a beanbag on selected body parts. Announce a color to identify those who are it.

Hand-eye coordination is slowly learned after many repetitions. Encourage students to repeat their attempts.

Game Activities

Midnight

Supplies: None

Skills: Running, dodging

A safety line is established about 40 ft from a den in which one player, the fox, is standing. The others stand behind the safety line and move forward slowly, asking, "Please, Mr. Fox, what time is it?" The fox answers in various fashions, such as "Bedtime," "Pretty late," "Three-thirty." The fox continues to draw the players toward him. At some point, he answers the question by saying "Midnight," and then chases the others back to the safety line. Any player who is caught joins the fox in the den and helps to catch others. No player in the den may leave, however, until the fox calls out "Midnight."

Variation: Lame Wolf. The wolf is lame and advances in a series of three running steps and a hop. Other children taunt, "Lame Wolf, can't catch me!" or "Lame Wolf, tame wolf, can't catch me!" The wolf may give chase at any time. Children who are caught join the wolf and must also move as if lame.

Teaching Hint: Learning to cooperate is a requisite for playing games. Very young students may not run because they want to be caught and be the center of attention. Tell those students that they will not be able to be the fox if they don't run.

Leap the Brook

Supplies: None

Skills: Leaping, jumping, hopping, turning

A brook is marked off on the floor for a distance of about 30 ft. For the first 10 ft, it is 3 ft wide; for the next 10 ft, it is 4 ft wide; for the last 10 ft, it is 5 ft wide. Children form a single file and jump over the narrowest part of the brook. They should be encouraged to do this several times, using different styles of jumping and leaping. After they have satisfactorily negotiated the narrow part, they move to the next width, and so on. The selection of the distances is arbitrary, and the distances can be changed if they seem unsuitable for any particular group of children.

Lesson Plans for Grades K-2 - Week 3
Fundamental Skills Using Hoops

Objectives:
To identify and perform the eight basic locomotor movements
To perform fitness challenges and understand what parts of the body are exercised
To manipulate the hoops
To understand simple rules of the games

Equipment Required:
Hoops (one per student)
Tom-tom or tambourine
Exercise tape (30 second intervals)

Instructional Activities	Teaching Hints

Introductory Activity --Locomotor Movements and Freeze

Perform the locomotor movements below; freeze quickly on signal with a wide base of support. A suggestion is to tape alternating segments of silence and music to signal duration of the locomotor movements. Segments of silence to indicate the "freeze" position can be decreased in duration until the desired response latency is reached.

1. Walk	5. Skip
2. Run	6. Gallop
3. Jump	7. Leap
4. Hop	8. Slide

Ask class to start moving upon entry into teaching area.

If necessary, demonstrate how to perform the movements.

Reinforce stopping without falling.

Fitness Development Activity --Movement Challenges

1. Locomotor Movement: Walk for 30 seconds.

2. Flexibility and Trunk Development Challenges
   a. Bend in different directions.
   b. Stretch slowly and return quickly.
   c. Combine bending and stretching movements.
   d. Sway back and forth.
   e. Twist one body part; add body parts.

3. Locomotor Movement: Skip for 30 seconds.

4. Shoulder Girdle Challenges
In a push-up position, do the following challenges:
   a. Lift one foot; the other foot.
   b. Wave at a friend; wave with the other arm.
   c. Scratch your back with one hand; use the other hand.
   d. Walk your feet to your hands.
   e. Turn over and face the ceiling; shake a leg; crab walk.

5. Locomotor Movement: Jog for 30 seconds.

6. Abdominal Development Challenges
From a supine position:
   1. Lift your head and look at your toes.
   2. Lift your knees to your chest.
   3. Wave your legs at a friend.
From a sitting position;
   1. Slowly lay down with hands on tummy.
   2. Lift legs and touch toes.

7. Locomotor Movement: Run and leap for 30 seconds.

Alternate the locomotor movements with the strength and flexibility challenges. Repeat the challenges as necessary.

Tape alternating segments (30 seconds in length) of silence and music to signal duration of exercise. Music segments indicate locomotor movements while intervals of silence announce doing the movement challenges.

Teach youngsters the different challenges and then allow them to select a challenge they can successfully perform.

The challenges should be enjoyable to perform.

Encourage students to focus on trying and feeling successful.

Workloads should be moderate with emphasis on success for all youngsters.

See text, p. 163-167 for descriptions of challenges.

Lesson Focus - Fundamental Skills Using Hoops

1. Stretch while standing inside your hoop.
   a. Different directions.
   b. Different parts of body.
2. Curl inside your hoop.
3. Balance with at least one body part in your hoop.
   a. Balance on different body parts.
   b. Balance on different number of parts.
   c. Go from one balance to another.
4. Make a bridge over your hoop.
   a. Bridge with feet in hoop and hands outside.
   b. Use different parts or number of parts.
5. Reach as far as possible.
   a. Keep toes in hoop, reach as far as possible.
   b. Keep hands in hoop, reach as far as possible.
6. Rock inside your hoop.
   a. On different sides of your body.
   b. Using different body parts.
7. Roll in and out of your hoop.
   a. Use different types of rolls.
   b. Roll up slowly into a small ball.
8. Twist inside your hoop.
   a. Do a large twist and hold it.
   b. Try moving slowly around your hoop and twisting.
   c. Twist and untwist at different speeds and levels.
9. Use other terms to explore fundamental skills.
   a. Straight, curved, narrow, wide, prone melt, shake, fall, collapse.

Perform Locomotor Movements In and Out of the Hoops
1. Use different locomotor movements- hop, jump, leap.
2. Place the majority of weight on the hands and perform Crouch jumps, forward and backward.
3. Do animal imitations, i.e., Rabbit, Frog, etc.
4. While doing locomotor movements: Add turns and jumps for height.
5. Do a combination of movements: Over one way and back another way.
6. See how many hoops you can jump in and out of in 10 seconds? Change the movements while moving between hoops.

Move around the Hoops
1. Try different locomotor movements.
2. Do Animal Walks, i.e., Dog, Bear, Cat, Rabbit.
3. Move around while keeping hands in the hoop.
4. Move around while keeping feet in the hoop.

Challenge Activities
1. Try some individual and partner stunts with the hoops as a base.
   a. Coffee Grinder - one hand in hoop on floor while moving around the hoop.
   b. Chinese Get-up - sit back to back in hoop with partner, hook elbows, and try to stand simultaneously.
   c. Wring the Dishrag
2. Jump from hoop to hoop without touching the floor. Can you move across the area? Skip from hoop to hoop.
3. Play "Ring around the hoop." Skip around the hoop and all fall down.
4. Move between five hoops and cartwheel through two hoops. Use different movements and tumbling activities.
5. Put your hoop together with a partner and make different shapes, numbers, and letters. Do the same thing in small groups.

This lesson teaches the fundamental locomotor and non-locomotor skills required for competent movement.

Each student has a hoop which serves as a home base for exploration and skill development.

Give students two or three activities to practice so you have time to move and help youngsters. Alternate activities from each of the categories so students receive a variety of skills to practice.

Don't become alarmed with students who haven't mastered all the movements such as skipping and galloping. Continue offering encouragement and many opportunities for practice. The skills will be learned in time.

Reinforce controlled movements. Encourage students to avoid falling and losing balance. Avoid reinforcing falling by laughing or calling attention to it.

If students become tired, change the activity or play one of the games at the end of this lesson. Hoop games can effectively pick up the interest and motivation of the class.

When offering challenges to students, make them open-ended, i.e., how many times can you...? Students have a tendency to think that if they did it once, they are finished. Instead, they should keep practicing the activity.

Use Back to Back or Whistle Mixer (see Lesson 1, p. 2) to get the students in partners.

Sneak Attack

    Supplies: None

    Skills: Marching, running

    Two parallel lines are drawn about 60 ft apart. Children are divided into two teams. One team takes a position on one of the lines, with their backs to the area. These are the chasers. The other team is on the other line, facing the area. This is the sneak team. The sneak team moves forward on signal, moving toward the chasers. When they get reasonably close, a whistle or some other signal is given, and the sneak team turns and runs back to their line, chased by the other team. Anyone caught before reaching the line changes to the chase team. The game is repeated, with the roles exchanged.

Teaching Hint: Use Back to Back or Whistle Mixer to get the students in partners. Then ask one partner to sit while the other stands. Send the stander to one team and the sitter to the other team.

    Students who choose not to run may not understand the importance of cooperating and following the rules. It might be necessary to discuss the importance of following rules so the game can be played.

Hoop Games

    Supplies: A hoop for each player

    Skills: Running, jumping

    Each child is seated in a hoop. On signal, each rises and jumps in and out of as many different hoops as possible. On the next signal, each child takes a seat inside the nearest hoop. The goal is to not be the last seated player. The game can also be played by eliminating one or two hoops so that one or two children are left without a home base. The first child to a hoop has ownership and gets to sit in it.

    A variation of this game is to have each child see how fast they can move through ten hoops and then return and sit in their designated hoop. A different challenge is to alternate touching a hoop and jumping in and out of a hoop until a total of ten is reached. Change the challenge as often as desired.

Teaching Hint:

It is a good idea to stipulate that students are not to slide into a hoop (This avoids accidents). The proper way is to run to the hoop and sit down in it. If youngsters do otherwise, play the game by having them place a hand on a hoop rather than sitting in it.

Lesson Plans for Grades K-2 - Week 4
Kicking, Trapping, Bowling, and Rolling Skills

Objectives:
To move and control a piece of equipment
To change speeds and directions of movement
To practice kicking, trapping, bowling and rolling skills
To successfully participate in simple games

Equipment Required:
One hoop for each student
Tom-tom
8" foam rubber ball (or 8½" partially
deflated playground ball) for each student
15 bowling pins

Instructional Activities	Teaching Hints

Introductory Activity -- Warm-up Activity Using Hoops

Issue a hoop for each child. Give them 2 to 3 minutes of free activity. If necessary, suggest some of the following challenges:
1. Run or hop with hoop, stop and jump the hoop.
2. Run and roll the hoop like a tire.
3. Spin the hoop and see how many time you can run around it.
4. Roll the hoop and go through it.
5. Combine two hoop activities with two locomotor movements.
6. Try some of the activities learned in the previous hoop lesson focus.

Ask class to start moving upon entry into teaching area.
Place the hoops around the perimeter of the area.

While the class is moving, ask students to acquire a hoop and practice jumping in and out of it. Reverse the procedure to put the hoops away.

Fitness Development Activity --Walk, Trot, and Jog

Move to the following signals:
1. One drumbeat - walk.
2. Two drumbeats - trot.
3. Three drumbeats - jog.
4. Whistle - freeze and perform exercises.

Perform various strength and flexibility exercises between bouts of walk, trot, and jog. Examples are:
1. Bend and Twist
2. Sitting Stretch
3. Push-up variations
4. Abdominal Challenges
5. Body Twist
6. Standing Hip Bend

Move around the perimeter of the area in the same direction.

Tape alternating segments (20 seconds in length) of silence and music to signal duration of exercise. Music segments indicate walk, trot, and jog activity. Intervals of silence signal performance of the strength and flexibility exercises.

See text, p. 174-186 for descriptions of exercises. Any exercises can be substituted. Try to maintain the balance of exercising all bodyparts.

Lesson Focus -- Kicking, Trapping, Rolling, and Bowling Skills

Kicking and Ball Control Skills

1. Inside of Foot Kick. Approach at 45° angle; inside of foot meets ball. Place non-kicking foot alongside ball.
2. Outside of Foot Kick. Short distance kick; keep toe down.
3. Long (instep) Pass. Contact the ball with the shoelaces. Not as accurate, but used for distance.
4. Sole of Foot Control. Use sole of foot to stop ball; make sure weight is placed on the non-receiving foot.
5. Inside of Foot Control. Use inside of foot and learn to "give" with leg so ball doesn't ricochet off foot.
6. Soccer skills can be practiced by the receiver. For example, the following skills are suggested:
   a. Toe Trap
   b. The Foot Pickup
   c. Bowl with Your Feet

Give each student a ball. The ball of preference is a 8" foam rubber ball since it will not be painful to kick and trap. Underinflated (they are easier to control) 8½" playground balls can be substituted.

Assign students two or three activities to practice so you have time to move and help youngsters. Alternate activities from each of the categories so students receive a variety of skills to practice.

Rolling and Bowling Skills

1. Two-handed roll; between the legs, with wide straddle stance.
2. Roll the ball with one hand. Use both left and right hands.
3. Roll the ball and put spin on the ball so it will curve to the left and right.
4. Roll the ball through human straddle targets:
   a. Start rolling at moderate stances and gradually increase as bowlers become more proficient.
   b. Use left and right hands.
   c. Scoring can be done giving two points for a ball that goes through the target without touching and one point for a ball going through, but touching a leg.
5. Use objects such as milk cartons, clubs, or bowling pins for targets. Various bowling games can be developed using the targets.
6. Stand with your back facing your partner. Bend over, look through your legs and bowl.

Work with a partner and practice rolling and bowling to each other.

When bowling through the legs of youngsters, students need to take turns. Encourage them to change position after three or four turns.

Game Activity

Change Sides

Supplies: None

Skill: Body management

Two parallel lines are established 30 ft apart. Half of the children are on each line. On signal, all cross to the other line, face the center, and stand at attention. The first group to do this correctly wins a point. Children must be cautioned to use care when passing through the opposite group. They should be spaced well along each line; this allows room for them to move through each group. The locomotor movements should be varied. The teacher may say, "Ready—walk!" Skipping, hopping, long steps, sliding, and other forms of locomotion can be specified. The position to be assumed at the finish can be varied also.

Variation: The competition can be by squads, with two squads on each line.

Teaching Hints: A primary goal of Change Sides is to learn to move through space without bumping into to others. If students are not moving under control, focus on body management rather than moving quickly.

Musical Ball Pass

Supplies: Playground ball per group, music

Skills: Passing and handling

Players stand in circle formation facing the center. One ball is given to a player and is passed to the circle players when the music starts. When the music stops, the player with the ball (or the last player to touch the ball) goes into the "well" in the center of the circle. The player in the well stays there until another player is caught with the ball.

Variation: More than one ball may be used, depending on the skill of the class.

Teaching Hint: Passes must be catchable. No batting of the ball is allowed. The ball must be caught before it can be tossed to the next person.

Lesson Plans for Grades K-2 - Week 5
Movement Skills and Concepts (Lesson 1)
Walking, Body Part Identification, and Personal Space

Objectives:
To run rhythmically
To jump a self-turned rope
To perform walking variations
To understand the concept of personal space

Equipment Required:
Tom-tom
One jump rope for each student
One balloon or beachball for each student

Instructional Activities	Teaching Hints
Introductory Activity - European Running	

1. Run and stop.
2. Run, and on signal make a full turn; continue in same direction. Turn the other way.
3. Run, and on signal run in general space. On next signal, re-form the original pattern.
4. Run and bend the upper body forward in four counts. Return to the upright position in four counts.
5. Run and clap the rhythm.

Stress personal space and moving without bumping into others.

Use a drum to accentuate the rhythm.

Start the rhythm slowly so students can hear and move easily. Accomplish a walking rhythm before moving to a trotting step.

Fitness Development Activity --Jump Rope Exercises

1. Jump rope - 45 seconds. If not able to jump, practice swinging the rope to the side while jumping
2. Place the rope on the floor and perform locomotor movements around and over the rope. Make different shapes and letters with the rope.
3. Hold the folded rope overhead. Sway from side to side. Twist right and left.
4. Jump rope - 45 seconds.
5. Lie on back with rope held with outstretched arms toward ceiling. Bring up one leg at a time and touch the rope with toes. Lift both legs together. Sit up and try to hook the rope over the feet. Release and repeat.
6. Touch toes with the folded rope.
7. Jump rope - 45 seconds.
8. Place rope on the floor and do various Animal Walks along or over the rope.
9. Do Push-up variations with the rope folded and held between the hands.
10. Jump rope - 45 seconds.

Tape alternating segments (45 seconds in length) of silence and music to signal duration of exercise. Music segments indicate aerobic activity with the jump ropes while intervals of silence announce using the jump ropes to enhance flexibility and strength development.

Teach youngsters to space themselves so they don't hit others with their rope.

Don't worry about non-jumpers. They will learn sooner or later. Give encouragement and keep them motivated.

Lesson Focus - Movement Skills and Concepts

Fundamental Skill: Walking
1. Walk in different directions, changing direction on signal (90°).
2. While walking, bring up the knees and slap with the hands on each step.
3. Walk on heels, toes, side of the foot, Charlie Chaplin fashion (toes pointed way out).
4. Gradually lower the body while walking; gradually raise body.
5. Walk with a smooth gliding step.
6. Walk with a wide base on tip-toes; rock from side to side.
7. Clap hands alternately front and back. Clap hands under the thighs (slow walk).
8. Walk slowly. Accelerate. Decelerate.
9. Take long strides. Tiny steps.
10. Change levels on signal.
11. Walk quickly and quietly. Slowly and heavily. Quickly and heavily, etc.
12. Change direction on signal while facing the same way.
13. Walk angrily, then happily; add others.
14. Hold arms in different positions. Try different arm movements as you walk.
15. Walk different patterns: circle, square, rectangle, figure-eight, etc.
16. Walk through heavy mud, on ice of slick floor on a rainy day.

Select a few activities from each of the categories so students receive a variety of skills to practice. When possible, integrate the manipulative skills activities with fundamental skill activities.

Use the instructional cues to help students walk with proper form. "Head up; eyes forward. Swing the arms while walking. Keep the shoulders back and the tummy flat"

A drumbeat can be used to stimulate different walking speeds.

17. Walk like a soldier, a giant, a robot; add other.
18. Duck under trees or railings while walking.
19. Point toes out in different directions while walking--in, forward, and out.
20. Walk with high knees, stiff knees, one stiff knee, sore ankle.
21. Walk toward a spot, turn around in four steps. Move in a different direction.
22. Practice changing steps while walking.
23. Walk with a military goose step.

Skills: Working with Balloons or Beachballs

1. Keep your balloon in the air by rebounding it from the hand, fist, arm, elbow, knee, shoulder, head, and other body parts. Use one finger. Use the feet to keep balloon in the air.
2. Work out combinations of body parts, four different parts in succession.
3. Use contrasting terms while keeping the balloon in the air:
   a. close—far
   b. in front of—behind
   c. near—far
   d. right—left
   e. high—low
   f. sudden--smooth
4. Keep one foot in place, control balloon or beachball.
5. Play "let's pretend" we are volleyball players. Practice overhand, underhand, dig passes. Show serving.
6. All time for exploratory activity by individuals or partners.

Keep the balloons in control by tapping them into the area rather than striking them.

When first learning the skills, keep the feet in one place rather than moving.

As children master the skills, try performing some of the balloon skills while moving throughout the area.

Movement Concept: Identifying Body Parts

1. Children can be standing or seated. Touch the part of parts with both hands without looking at it. Children should repeat out loud the designated part touched by saying, "I am touching _____."
   a. Touch your shoulders
   b. Touch your ankles
   c. Touch your head
   d. Touch your toes
   e. Touch your ears
   f. Touch your knees
   g. Touch your eyes
   h. Touch your hips
   i. Touch your cheeks
   j. Touch your forehead
   k. Touch your thighs
   l. Touch your elbows
2. Thinking Activity
   Teacher touches the incorrect part of the body as commands are given. Students should touch the correct part and not be fooled by the teacher
3. As a part is named, form a pose and make this part the highest position of your body; the lowest.
4. Move about general space in any manner you wish. When a body part is called, stop and put both hands on the part(s).
5. Select a way you wish to move in general space. The signal to move will be the name of a body part. Move around the room with one hand on the body part. When another body part is called out, change the type of movement and hold the new body part.

Body part identification should be a "snappy" activity. Children should learn to respond quickly without much thought.

Practice combinations of body parts such as shoulders-ankles and knees.

Try the activities with the eyes closed.

Movement Concept: Exploring Personal Space

1. Keeping one foot in place on a spot, make a full arc with the other foot. Keep both one foot and one hand touching the spot, arc again with other foot.
2. Keeping your feet in place, sway and reach out as far as you can without losing balance or moving feet. Try with feet together and feet apart. Which is better for balance? Sit down and repeat movements. Do you need more or less space?

Place emphasis on understanding that most people have a personal space they don't want violated. Encourage youngsters to stay out of other's personal spaces.

3. Try some different types of movements in your personal space:

   a. Make yourself as wide as possible. Change to narrow. Experiment with narrow, small--large, high--low, etc. Try from other positions--kneeling, sitting balancing of seat, standing on one foot, lying on stomach, and other.

   b. In supine position, move arms and legs in different combinations out and back.

   c. Select one part of the body to keep in place. Make big circles with the rest of the body. Select other parts.

   d. Explore different positions where one foot is higher than any other body part.

   e. Pump yourself up like a balloon. Get bigger and bigger until I say, "Pop!"

   f. Let's pretend you are a snowman melting to the ground under a hot sun.

   g. With your feet in place, twist as far as you can one way and then the other (arms out to sides). Show me how a top spins.

Call out different movements and encourage students to respond quickly.

Offer the activities as challenges and allow students to do their best.

Game Activity

Jack Frost and Jane Thaw

   Supplies: Any type of marker to distinguish Jack Frost, and Jane Thaw

   Skills: Running, dodging, holding position

   Children are scattered and move to avoid being frozen (tagged) by Jack Frost. Frozen children must remain immobile until touched (thawed) by Jane Thaw. Freezing occurs instantly, but thawing is a more gradual process. Two Jack Frosts can help keep the action moving.

Marching Ponies

   Supplies: None

   Skills: Marching, running

   One child, the ringmaster, crouches in the center of a circle of ponies formed by the other children. Two goal lines on opposite sides of the circle are established as safe areas. The ponies march around the circle in step, counting as they do so. At a predetermined number (whispered to the ringmaster by the teacher), the ringmaster jumps up and attempts to tag the others before they can reach the safety lines. Anyone tagged joins the ringmaster in the center and helps catch the other children the next time. The game should be reorganized after six to eight children have been caught. Those left in the circle are declared the winners.

Variation: Other characterizations, such as lumbering elephants, jumping kangaroos, and the like, can be tried. A child who suggests a unique movement could be allowed to be the ringmaster.

Tag Games

   Supplies: None

   Skills: Fundamental locomotor movements, dodging

   Tag is played in many ways. Children are scattered about the area. One child is it and chases the others, trying to tag one of them. When a tag is made, she says, "You're it." The new it chases other children.

Variations:

   1. Object Tag. Touching a specified type of object (e.g., wood, iron) or the floor or an object of a specified color makes the runner safe.

   2. Mimic Tag. Children can be safe by mimicking a particular action or pose.

   3. Locomotor Tag. The child who is it specifies how the others should move--skipping, hopping, jumping. The tagger must use the same kind of movement.

  4. Frozen Tag. Two children are it. The rest are scattered over the area. When caught, they are "frozen" and must keep both feet in place. Any free player can tag a frozen player and thus release her. The goal of the tagger is to freeze all players. Frozen players can be required to hop in place until released.

Lesson Plans for Grades K-2 - Week 6
Rhythmic Movement (Lesson 1)

Objectives:
To be able to identify and perform animal movements
To march individually and in patterns
To be able to move rhythmically
To perform simple folk dances

Equipment Required:
Records for folk dances
Parachute
Magic Number cards
Playground ball for game

Instructional Activities	Teaching Hints

Introductory Activity -- Magic Number Challenges

Students put together a series of movements based on the magic numbers given. For example, hold up a card with three numbers on it (10, 8, 14). Students respond by performing three different locomotor movements the specified number of times, respectively.

Encourage variety of response.

Use movements such as walking, running, jumping, hopping, galloping, sliding, leaping, and skipping.

Fitness Development Activity --Animal Movements and Fitness Challenges

1. Puppy Dog Walk–30 seconds.
2. Freeze; perform stretching activities.
3. Lion Walk--30 seconds
4. Freeze; perform abdominal development challenges.
5. Seal Walk–30 seconds.
6. Freeze; perform push-up position challenges.
7. Elephant Walk–30 seconds.
8. Injured Coyote Walk—30 seconds.
9. Freeze; perform abdominal challenges.
10. Crab Walk—30 seconds.
11. Rabbit Jump

Tape alternating segments (30 seconds in length) of silence and music to signal duration of exercise. Music segments indicate performing animal movements while intervals of silence announce doing the fitness challenges.

A variation is to place animal movement signs throughout the area and instruct students to move from sign to sign performing the appropriate animal movement each time they reach a new sign.

Lesson Focus - Rhythmic Movement (1)

Marching
Try the following sequence:
1. Clap hands while standing in place to the beat of a tom-tom or record.
2. March in place; always start with the left foot.
3. March to the music in scatter formation, adding some of the following challenges;
   a Be a big or small as you can.
   b Count the rhythm.
   c Change direction on signal.
   d March backwards.
   e March loudly or quietly.
   f Make up a rhythmic poem like "Sound Off."
   g. Be a drum major leading the band.
   h. Play various instruments in the band while marching.
4. Try some simple patterns such as the following:
   a Single-line formation.
   b Double-line formation (with a partner).
   c Two lines meet and go up the center.
   d Two lines meet and split on signal.
   e Make up your own formation

Alternate activities from each of the categories so students receive a variety of skills to practice.

Use scatter formation during early learning stages.

When march in line, try to maintain spacing between individuals.

If desired, teach commands such as "about face, forward march, and halt."

Try saluting each other as they march past.

Parachute Rhythmic Routine

Perform rhythmic activities while holding or manipulating the parachute:

Beats	Movement
1-8	Eight walking steps to the left. Hold chute in both hands.
9-16	Eight backward steps to the right.
17-20	Raise parachute above head (up-2-3-4).
21-24	Lower chute to floor (Down-2-3-4).
25-32	Shake the chute (Up and Down).
33-36	Raise the chute overhead.
37-44	Lower chute quickly to floor and form a dome. Hold the dome for eight beats.

Practice the steps without the parachute when learning the movements.

Instead of holding to a specified number of beats, it might be easier to call out a change. This allows the teacher to continue the movement until most students have learned.

Rhythmic Activities

Make dances easy for students to learn by implementing some of the following techniques:

1. Teach the dances without using partners.
2. Allow youngsters to move in any direction without left-right orientation.
3. Use scattered formation instead of circles.
4. Emphasize strong movements such as clapping and stamping to increase involvement.
5. Play the music at a slower speed when first learning the dance.

Rhythms should be taught like other sport skills. Avoid striving for perfection so students know it is acceptable to make mistakes. Teach a variety of dances rather than one or two in depth in case some students find it difficult to master a specific dance. Records can be ordered from Wagon Wheel Records, 17191 Corbina Lane #203, Huntington Beach, CA (714) 846-8169.

Movin' Madness (American)

Records: LS E-9, E-20; MAV 1044, 1041; AR 572
Formation: Scattered
Directions:
Part I:
The tempo is slow, slow, fast-fast-fast. The children do any series of movements of their choice to fit this pattern, repeated four times. The movements should be large, gross motor movements.
Part II:
During the second part (chorus) of the music, the children do any locomotor movement in keeping with the tempo. The step-hop or a light run can be used with the tempo of Part II.
Teaching suggestions: Have the youngsters clap the rhythm. They should pay particular attention to the tempo in Part I. The music is Bleking, a dance presented later. The music for "I See You" is also suitable, but note that the movements in Part I are repeated twice instead of four times. The Part II music is suitable for skipping, sliding, or galloping.

Did You Ever See a Lassie? (Scottish)

Records: LS E-4; CM-1 1157
Formation: Single circle, facing halfway left, with hands joined; one child in the center

Directions:
Measures Action

Measures	Action
1--8	All walk (one step per measure) to the left in a circle with hands joined. (Walk, 2, 3, 4, 5, 6, 7, 8) The child in the center gets ready to demonstrate some type of movement.
9--16	All stop and copy the movement suggested by the child in the center.

As the verse starts over, the center child selects another to do some action in the center and changes places with her.

Let Your Feet Go Tap, Tap, Tap (German)

Records: LS E-7, E-20
Formation: Double circle, partners facing
Directions:
Action
Tap the foot three times. (Tap, 2, 3)
Clap the hands three times. (Clap, 2, 3)
Beckon and bow to partner. (Beckon, bow)
Join inside hands and face counterclockwise. (Join hands)

Chorus

All skip counterclockwise.

If children are having difficulty with skipping, substitute a walking, running, or sliding step.

Ach Ja (German)

Records: LS E-2; CM 1158

Formation: Double circle, partners facing counterclockwise, partners A on the inside, inside hands joined

Directions:

Explain that "Ach Ja" means "Oh yes."

Measures	*Action*
1--2	Partners walk eight steps in the line of direction. (Walk, 2, 3, 4, 5, 6, 7, 8)
3	Partners drop hands and bow to each other. (Bow)
4	Each A then bows to the B on the left, who returns the bow. (Bow)
5--8	Measures 1--4 are repeated.
9--10	Partners face each other, join hands, and take four slides in the line of direction. (Slide, 2, 3, 4)
11--12	Four slides are taken clockwise. (Slide, 2, 3, 4)
13	Partners bow to each other. (Bow)
14	A bows to the B on the left, who returns the bow. (Bow) To start the next dance, A moves quickly toward this B, who is the next partner.

Game Activity

Squirrel in the Trees

Supplies: None

Skills: Fundamental locomotor movements

A number of trees are formed by two players facing each other and holding hands or putting hands on each other's shoulders. A squirrel is in the center of each tree, and one or two extra squirrels are outside. On signal, all squirrels move out of their tree and move around the area. The paired players (trees) also move while holding hands. On a second signal, the squirrels find another tree trying not to be an extra without a tree. Only one squirrel is allowed in a tree.

Teaching suggestion: Rotate periodically so all youngsters are able to be squirrels. Rotate by having the squirrels face one tree person. The person with their back to the squirrel becomes the new squirrel.

Stop Ball

Supplies: A ball

Skills: Tossing, catching

One child, with hands over the eyes, stands in the center of a circle of children. A ball is tossed clockwise or counterclockwise from child to child around the circle. Failing to catch the ball or making a bad toss incurs a penalty. That child must take one long step back and stay out of the game for one turn.

At a time of her own selection, the center player calls, "Stop." The player caught with the ball steps back and stays out for one turn. The center player should be allowed three or four turns and then be changed.

Lesson Plans for Grades K-2 - Week 7
Long-Rope Jumping Skills

Objectives:
To perform locomotor movements on cue
To choose fitness activities that assure personal success
To perform long jump roping skills
To know the difference between front and back door entry in long rope jumping
To pass and catch balls in a game setting

Equipment Required:
Circuit training signs and cones
One long jump rope per 4-6 students (12-16 ft in length)
One 9 ft jump rope for students who have trouble turning the rope
5 or 6 balls for game activities

Instructional Activities	Teaching Hints
Introductory Activity --Crossing the River	
A river is designated by two lines about 40 feet apart. Each time the youngsters cross the river the must perform a different movement. For example:	Stress quality of movement, not speed.
1. Run, walk, hop, skip, leap.	Reinforce creativity and original
2. Animal Walks such as bear, crab, and puppy dog.	movements.
3. Partner run, back to back, side by side.	

Fitness Development Activity -- Circuit Training	
Make signs, put them on cones and place around the perimeter of the teaching area. Students perform the exercise specified at each station while the music is playing.	Tape alternating segments of silence and music to signal duration of exercise. Music segments (begin at 30 seconds) indicate activity at each station while intervals of silence (10 seconds) announce it is time to stop and move forward to the next station.
1. Tortoise and Hare	
2. Curl-up variations	
3. Hula Hooping on arms	
4. Standing Hip Bend	
5. Agility run--run back and forth between two designated lines	
6. Push-up variations	See text, p. 174-186 for descriptions of exercises.
7. Crab Walk	
8. Bend and Twist	

Lesson Focus - Long-Rope Jumping Skills	
1. Jump a stationary rope, gradually raise the rope.	Groups of four students work best because it allows students to rotate easily (two turners and two jumpers) without anyone being left out.
2. Ocean Waves--Shake the rope with an up-and-down motion. Students try to jump a "low spot."	
3. Snake in the grass--Wiggle the rope back and forth on the grass. Jump without touching the rope.	
4. Pendulum swing--Move the rope back and forth like a pendulum. Jump the rope as it approaches the jumper.	Use shorter jump ropes for students who have trouble learning to turn.
5. Practice turning the rope with a partner. The skill of turning *must* precede jumping skills. Standard 16 ft. long ropes are difficult for young children to turn. Substitute 8 to 12 ft ropes depending on the maturity of the youngsters.	Teach turning by having students hold an end of the rope and standing as far apart as possible. Make small circles with the rope and gradually step toward each other, making large circles.
6. Practice turning the rope to rhythm. Music with a strong beat or a steady tom-tom beat is useful for developing rhythmic turning. Turning the rope to a steady rhythm *must* precede jumping skills.	
7. Run through a turning rope.	
8. Stand in the center of the turners and jump the rope as it is turned once. Add more jumps.	Rhythmic turning is important! Many students miss the jump because of erratic turning. Practice turning until it becomes a smooth even tempo.
9. Run in, jump once, and run out.	
10. Front door--turn the rope toward the jumper.	
11. Try the following variations:	
a Run in front door and out back door.	Allow beginners to tell the turners what activity they want to do. Self-choice helps assure success.
b Run in back door and out front door.	
c. Run in back door and out back door.	
d. Run in front or back door, jump a specified number of times, and out.	
e. Run in front or back door, jump, and do a quarter, half, and full turn in the air.	
f. Turn around while jumping.	

12. Recite a chant while jumping.

Examples of chants:
Tick tock, tick tock,
What's the time by the clock?
It's one, two, [up to midnight].

I like coffee, I like tea,
How many people can jump like me?
One, two, three, [up to a certain number].

Game Activity

Ball Passing

Supplies: Five or six different kinds of balls for each circle
Skill: Object handling

The class is divided into two or more circles, with no more than 15 children in any one circle. Each circle consists of two or more squads, but squad members need not stand together.

The teacher starts a ball around the circle; it is passed from player to player in the same direction. The teacher introduces more balls until five or six are moving around the circle at the same time and in the same direction. If a child drops a ball, he must retrieve it, and a point is scored against his squad. After a period of time, a whistle is blown, and the points against each squad are totaled. The squad with the lowest score wins. Beanbags, large blocks, or softballs can be substituted for balls.

Hot Potatoes

Supplies: One to three balls or beanbags for each group
Skill: Object handling

Children are seated in small circles (8 to 12 per circle) so that objects can be passed from one to another around the circle. Balls or beanbags or both are passed around the circle. The teacher or a selected student looks away from the class and randomly shouts, "stop!" The point of the game is to avoid getting stuck with an object. If this happens, the player(s) with an object must get up and move to the next circle. The teacher should begin the game with one object and gradually add objects if the class is capable.
Variation: The passing direction can be reversed on signal.

Aviator

Supplies: None
Skills: Running, locomotor movements, stopping

Players are parked (in push-up position) at one end of the playing area. The air traffic controller (ATC) is in front of the players and calls out, "Aviators aviators, take off!" Youngsters take off and move like airplanes to the opposite side of the area. The first person to move to the other side and land the plane (get into push-up position facing the ATC) is declared the new ATC.

If the ATC yells out some type of stormy weather, all planes must return to the starting line and resume the parked position. Examples of stormy weather commands are lightning, thunder, hurricane, and tornado. Each ATC is allowed to give stormy weather warnings once.

Lesson Plans for Grades K-2 - Week 8
Manipulative Skills Using Playground Balls

Objectives:
To perform combinations of locomotor and non-locomotor movements
To bounce, toss, and catch a ball in a stationary position
To roll, bounce, and throw a ball to a partner.

Equipment Required:
One 8½" playground ball for each
   student
Tom-tom

Instructional Activities	Teaching Hints

Introductory Activity -- Combination Movements

1. Hop, turn around, and shake.
2. Jump, make a shape in the air, balance.
3. Skip, collapse, and roll.
4. Curl, roll, jump with a half turn.
5. Whirl, skip, sink slowly.
6. Hop, collapse, creep.
7. Kneel, sway, jump to feet.
8. Lift, grin, and roll.

Use the tom-tom to signal movement changes.

Challenge students to develop their personal combinations.

Create different movements using the same words.

Fitness Development Activity -- Fitness Challenges

Alternate locomotor movements with strength and flexibility challenges. Repeat the challenges as necessary.

Locomotor Movement: Walk for 30 seconds.

Flexibility and Trunk Development Challenges
1. Bend in different directions.
2. Stretch slowly and return quickly.
3. Combine bending and stretching movements.
4. Sway back and forth.
5. Twist one body part; add body parts.
6. Make your body move in a large circle.
7. In a sitting position, wave your legs at a friend; make circles with your legs.

Locomotor Movement: Skip for 30 seconds.

Shoulder Girdle Challenges
In a push-up position, do the following challenges:
1. Lift one foot; the other foot.
2. Wave at a friend; wave with the other arm.
3. Scratch your back with one hand; use the other hand.
4. Walk your feet to your hands.
5. Turn over and face the ceiling; shake a leg; Crab Walk.

Locomotor Movement: Jog for 30 seconds.

Abdominal Development
From a supine position:
1. Lift your head and look at your toes.
2. Lift your knees to your chest.
3. Wave your legs at a friend. From a sitting position:
1. Slowly lay down with hands on tummy.
2. Lift legs and touch toes.

Locomotor Movement: Run and leap for 30 seconds.

Tape alternating segments (30 seconds in length) of silence and music to signal duration of exercise. Music segments indicate doing the locomotor movements while intervals of silence announce performing the strength and flexibility challenges

See text, p. 163-167 for descriptions of challenges.

Students select a fitness challenge they feel capable of performing. This implies that not all youngsters are required to do the same workload. Children differ and their ability to perform fitness workloads differs. Make fitness a personal challenge.

Since the range of activities is from easy to challenging, all youngsters can be successful. All youngsters should be able to do one of the fitness challenges.

Vary the locomotor movements as desired. Another alternative is to allow students to select the locomotor movement they would like to do.

Lesson Focus -- Manipulative Skills Using Playground Balls

1. Controlled Rolling and Handling in Place
   a. In a wide straddle position (other possible positions are seated with legs crossed or outstretched, and push-up position), place the ball on the floor, and roll it with constant finger guidance between and around the legs.
   b. Roll the ball in a figure-eight path in and out of the legs.
   c. Reach as far to the left as possible with the ball and roll it in front of you to the other side. Catch it as far to the right of the body as possible.
   d. Turn in place and roll the ball around with one hand in a large circle.
   e. Roll the ball around while lying on top of it. Roll the ball around the floor while on all fours, guiding it with the nose and forehead.
   f. With the back moderately bent, release the ball behind the head, let it roll down the back, and catch it with both hands.
   g. Make different kinds of bridges over the ball while using the ball as partial support for the bridge.

   Give students two or three activities to practice so you have time to move and help youngsters. Alternate activities from each of the categories so students receive a variety of activities for practice.

   Place emphasis on control of the ball. Students should challenged to have "their ball under control."

2. Bounce and Catch
   a. Two hands, one hand.
   b. Bounce at different levels.
   c. Bounce between legs.
   d. Close eyes and bounce.
   e. Dribble ball in a stationary and/or moving position.
   f. Dribble and follow the commands, such as move forward, backward, in a circle, or sideways, while walking, galloping, trotting, etc.
   g. Exploratory activity.

   An effective approach is to tell students to assume their feet are "glued to the floor." Tosses must be made directly overhead and caught without moving.

3. Toss and Catch
   a. Toss and catch, vary height.
   b. Add various challenges while tossing (i.e., touch floor, clap hands, turn, sit down, lie down).
   c. Toss and let bounce. Also add some challenges as above.
   d. Toss up and catch behind back--toss from behind back and catch in front of body.
   e. Create moving challenges (i.e., toss, run five steps and catch, toss and back up five hops and catch.)
   f. Exploratory activity.

   Tosses must begin at a low level and gradually be raised as students gain control of the ball. Little is gained by tossing the ball to a height where it can't be caught.

4. Foot Skills
   a. Lift the ball up with both feet and catch. Both front and rear of body catch.
   b. From a sitting position with the ball between feet, toss it up, and catch with hands.
   c. Keep the ball in the air with feet and different body parts.

Game Activity

Teacher Ball

Supplies: A gray foam ball or rubber playground ball

Skills: Throwing, catching

One child is the teacher or leader and stands about 10 ft in front of three other students, who are lined up facing him. The object of the game is to move up to the teacher's spot by avoiding making bad throws or missing catches. The teacher throws to each child in turn, beginning with the child on the left, who must catch and return the ball. Any child making a throwing or catching error goes to the end of the line, on the teacher's right. Those in the line move up, filling the vacated space.

If the teacher makes a mistake, he must go to the end of the line and the child at the head of the line becomes the new teacher. The teacher scores a point by remaining in position for three rounds (three throws to each child). After scoring a point, the teacher takes a position at the end of the line and another child becomes the teacher.

Teaching suggestion: This game should be used only after children have a minimal competency in throwing and catching skills. It can be a part of the skill-teaching program.

Variation: The teacher can suggest specific methods of throwing and catching, such as "Catch with the right hand only" or "Catch with one hand and don't let the ball touch your body."

The Scarecrow and the Crows

Supplies: None

Skills: Dodging, running

Children form a large circle representing the garden, which one child, designated the scarecrow, guards. From six to eight crows scatter on the outside of the circle, and the scarecrow assumes a characteristic pose inside the circle. The circle children raise their joined hands and let the crows run through, into the garden, where they pretend to eat. The scarecrow tries to tag the crows. The circle children help the crows by raising their joined hands and allowing them to leave the circle, but they try to hinder the scarecrow. If the scarecrow runs out of the circle, all the crows immediately run into the garden and start to nibble at the vegetables, while the circle children hinder the scarecrow's reentry.

When the scarecrow has caught one or two crows, a new group of children is selected. If, after a reasonable period of time, the scarecrow has failed to catch any crows, a change should be made.

Lesson Plans for Grades K-2 - Week 9
Movement Skills and Concepts Using Jump Rope Patterns

Objectives:
To be able to quickly distinguish between bending, stretching and shaking
To be able to exhibit cooperation in simple tag games
To perform locomotor movements using a rope as a prop
To jump a self-turned rope

Equipment Required:
Tambourine
Music for rope jumping
One individual jump rope for each child

Instructional Activities	Teaching Hints
Introductory Activity -- Bend, Stretch, and Shake	
1. Bend various body parts individually and then bend various combinations of body parts.	Use a tambourine to signal changes between bending, stretching and shaking.
2. Stretch the body in various levels. Encourage stretching from various positions such as standing, sitting, and prone position.	
3. Practice shaking individual body parts when the tambourine is shaken. Progress to shaking the entire body.	Encourage smooth movements in bending and stretching activities.
4. Bend body parts while doing different locomotor movements. Bend limbs while shaking.	
	Encourage creative responses.
Fitness Development Activity -- Fitness Games and Challenges	
1. Stoop Tag - 45 seconds.	Tape alternating segments of silence and
2. Freeze; perform stretching activities.	music to signal duration of exercise.
3. Back-to-Back Tag - 45 seconds.	Music segments indicate fitness game
4. Freeze; perform Abdominal Challenges using Curl-up variations.	activity while intervals of silence
5. Balance Tag - 45 seconds.	announce flexibility and strength
6. Freeze; perform Arm-Shoulder Girdle Challenges using Push-up variations.	development activities.
7. Elbow Swing Tag - 45 seconds.	
8. Freeze; perform Trunk Development challenges.	See text, p. 168-169 for descriptions of
9. Color Tag - 45 seconds.	tag games. The names of the tag games indicate a "safe" position when one cannot be tagged, i.e., back to back with a partner or balancing on one foot.
	Avoid getting caught up in rule infractions. The purpose of the tag games is to encourage locomotor movement.
Lesson Focus - Movement Skills and Concepts Using Rope Patterns	
A. Rope Patterns	Alternate rope pattern activities with rope
Lay rope lengthwise on floor.	jumping activities. This offers students
1. Walk as on a balance beam.	time for recovery after rope jumping.
a. Forward	
b. Backward	
c. Sideways	
2. Jump/hop down length and back.	Encourage using both sides of the body.
a. Vary time--slow, fast, accelerate, decelerate, even, uneven	If hopping on the right foot, give equal
b. Vary levels and force--light, heavy, high to low.	time to the left foot.
3. Other locomotor movements.	
a. Crisscross	
b. Jumps with one-half turn	
c. Allow student choice	If youngsters have trouble jumping or
4. Imitate animals.	hopping over the rope, encourage them to
5. Crouch jumps.	step or leap over.
a. Various combinations; forward, backward, sideways.	
b. Allow exploration.	Select some children to demonstrate a
6. Put rope in shapes, letters, numbers.	movement shape or letter. When asking
a. Move in and out of figures.	students to demonstrate, be sure they are
b. Add movements, keeping the body inside figure.	capable to avoid embarrassment.

7. Partner work.
    a. Make figure with two ropes. Move in and out of figure.
    b. Using one rope, do follow activity. Take turns.

B. Rope Jumping
1. Hold rope. Jump in time.
2. Perform the slow-time and fast-time rhythm with the rope held in one hand and turned (propellers).
3. Jump the rope and practice slow to fast time.
4. Introduce a few basic steps.
    a. Two-step basic
    b. Alternating basic
    c. Backwards
    d. One foot

This lesson should introduce youngsters to rope jumping. It should not be too instructional, but should be used for the purpose of giving them a positive introduction to rope jumping. Instruction will come in a later lesson.

Game Activity

Charlie Over the Water
Supplies: A volleyball or playground ball
Skills: Skipping, running, stopping, bowling (rolling)
The children are in circle formation with hands joined. One child, Charlie (or Sally, if a girl), is in the center of the circle, holding a ball. The children skip around the circle to the following chant.
Charlie over the water,
Charlie over the sea,
Charlie caught a bluebird,
But he can't catch me!
On the word "me," Charlie tosses the ball in the air and children drop hands and scatter. When Charlie catches it, he shouts "Stop!" All of the children stop immediately and must not move their feet. Charlie rolls the ball in an attempt to hit one of the children. If he hits a child, that child becomes the new Charlie. If he misses, he must remain Charlie, and the game is repeated. If he misses twice, however, he picks another child for the center.

Flowers and Wind
Supplies: None
Skill: Running
Two parallel lines long enough to accommodate the children are drawn about 30 ft apart. Children are divided into two groups. One is the wind and the other the flowers. Each of the teams takes a position on one of the lines and faces the other team. The flowers secretly select the name of a common flower. When ready, they walk over to the other line and stand about 3 ft away from the wind. The players on the wind team begin to call out flower names--trying to guess the flower chosen. When the flower has been guessed, the flowers run to their goal line, chased by the players of the other team. Any player caught must join the other side. The roles are reversed and the game is repeated. If one side has trouble guessing, a clue can be given to the color or size of the flower or the first letter of its name.

Lesson Plans for Grades K-2 - Week 10
Movement Skills and Concepts
Jumping, Tossing and Catching, and Moving in General Space

Objectives:
To learn to evade or follow a partner while moving under control in general space
To learning a variety of jumping skills
To learn how forceful movements are generated

Equipment Required:
One yarn ball for each student
Tom-tom or tambourine
Parachute

Instructional Activities	Teaching Hints

Introductory Activity -- Marking

Find a partner. One person attempts to evade the other. The goal is to try to lose the person attempting to stay near. On the command "freeze," students stop and try to "mark" by touching partner. If the partner is too far away to touch, no "mark" is scored. Reverse and allow the other partner to evade.
Variations:

1. Use the eight basic locomotor movements.
2. Use positions such as Crab Walk, Puppy Dog Walk, etc.
3. Allow a point to be scored only when they touch a specified body part, i.e., knee, elbow, left hand.
4. Use a whistle signal to change partners' roles. (If chasing partner, reverse and attempt to move *away* from the other.)

Run under control. Students should be taught to never run as fast as possible. Running and being able to stop quickly will help avoid collisions.

Change partners once or twice.

Use animal walks if students cannot run under control.

Fitness Development Activity --Parachute Fitness

1. Jog while holding the chute in the left hand. (music)
2. Shake the chute. (no music)
3. Slide while holding the chute with both hands. (music)
4. Sit and perform curl-ups - (no music)
5. Skip. (music)
6. Freeze, face the center, and stretch the chute tightly. Hold for 8-12 seconds. Repeat five to six times. (no music)
7. Run in place while holding the chute taut at different levels. (music)
8. Sit with legs under the chute. Do a seat walk toward the center. Return to the perimeter. Repeat four to six times. (no music)
9. Place the chute on the ground. Jog away from the chute and return on signal. Repeat. (music)
10. Move into push-up position holding the chute with one hand. Shake the chute. (no music)
11. Shake the chute and jump in place. (music)
12. Lie on back with feet under the chute. Shake the chute with the feet. (no music)
13. Hop to the center of the chute and return. Repeat. (music)
14. Sit with feet under the chute. Stretch by touching the toes with the chute. Relax with other stretches while sitting. (no music)

Tape alternating segments (20 seconds in length) of silence and music to signal duration of exercise. Music segments indicate aerobic activity with the parachute while intervals of silence announce using the chute to enhance flexibility and strength development.

Space youngsters evenly around the chute.

Use different hand grips (palms up, down, mixed).

All movements should be done under control. Some of the faster and stronger students will have to moderate their performance.

Lesson Focus -- Movement Skills and Concepts (2)

Fundamental Skill--Jumping

1. Jump upward, trying for height.
2. Alternate low and high jumps.
3. Jump in various floor patterns--triangle, circle, square, letters, figure-eight, diamond shape.
4. Over a spot, jump forward, backwards, sideways, criss-cross.
5. Jump with the body stiff, like a pogo stick. Explore with arms in different positions.
6. Practice jump turns--quarter, half, three-quarter, full. Add heel clicks with turns.
7. Increase and decrease the speed of jumping. Increase the height of jumping.
8. Land with the feet apart sideways and together again. Try it forward and backward (stride).
9. Jump and land as quietly as possible.

Select a few activities from each of the categories so students receive a variety of skills to practice. When possible, integrate the manipulative skill activities with fundamental skill activities. A common error is to teach all the activities from one category. The reason for multiple groups of activities is to provide variety and enhance motivation.

Use instructional cues such as:

10. Jump and criss-cross the feet sideways.
11. See how far you can jump in two, three, or four consecutive jumps.
12. Pretend you are a bouncing ball.
13. Clap hands or slap thighs when in the air.
14. Jump so the hands contact the floor.
15. Select a line. Proceed down it by jumping back and forth over the line. Add turns.

"Swing your arms forward as you jump"

"Bend your knees"

"Land lightly by bending your knees"

"Jump as high as you can"

Manipulative Activity: Yarn Balls
Individual Activity
1. Toss and catch to self.
    a. Increase height gradually.
    b. Side to side.
    c. Front to back.
    d. Toss underneath the legs, around the body, etc.
    e. Toss and clap the hands. Clap around the body. Underneath the legs.
    f. Toss and make turns--quarter and half.
    g. Toss and perform the following challenges while ball is in air: Heel click, touch both elbows, knees, shoulders, and heels.
    h. Use contrasting tosses such as: High and low, near and far, front and back.
2. Bat the ball upward as in volleyball, catch. Bat the ball, run forward and catch.
3. Toss forward, run and catch. Toss sideways and catch. Toss overhead, turn around, run and catch.

Have the yarn balls placed around the perimeter of the area. On signal, ask students to jog to a ball, pick it up and practice tossing and catching.

Toss the ball to a height where it can be caught. Little is gained by a toss which is too high and out of control.

Partner Activity
1. Roll the ball back and forth.
2. Toss the ball back and forth, various ways.
3. Throw the ball back and forth.

Encourage a successful toss to be one where the feet do not have to be moved to make a catch.

Movement Concept: Moving in General Space
1. Run lightly in the area, changing direction as you wish without bumping or touching anyone. How many were able to do this? Try running zigzag fashion.
2. Run again in general space. On signal, change direction abruptly. Try again, only this time change both direction and the type of locomotor movement you are doing.
3. Run lightly and pretend you are dodging another runner. Run directly at another runner and dodge him or her.
4. Use a yarn ball to mark your personal space (spot); run in general space until the signal is given; return to your yarn ball and sit down.
5. We are going to do orienteering. Point to a spot on a wall, walk directly to the spot in a straight line. You may have to wait for other so as not to bump them. Pick another spot on a different wall and repeat. Return to home base on signal.
6. What happens when general space is decreased? Walk in general space. Now as space is decreased, walk again. Once more we are decreasing the space.
7. Run around your yarn ball until I Say, "Bang." Then explode in a straight direction until the stop signal is sounded. Return.
8. From your spot, take three (four or five) jumps (hops, skips, gallops, slides) in one direction, turn around and do the same back to home base. Try with long steps away and tiny steps back.
9. I am going to challenge you on right and left movements. First, let's walk in general space. When I say "right" (or "left") you change direction abruptly.
10. This time run rapidly toward another child. Stop and bow. Now stop and shake hands.

Partners should start close together and gradually move apart as they become successful.

Place the yarn ball on the floor and used them as objects to move over and around.

Dodging demands running under control. Students should seldom run as fast as possible in physical education classes. Most activities demand controlled movement.

Explain simple orienteering activity.

Movement Concept: Use of Force
1. Show us how you do some forceful movements, such as chopping batting, hitting with a sledge, hitting a punching bag. Try karate chops and kicks, kicking a soccerball, etc.

2. Show us a light movement you can make with the arm. Repeat the same movement more forcefully.
3. Make some movements that are light and sustained, heavy and sudden, heavy and sustained, light and sudden.
4. Make one part of the body move lightly, while another moves heavily.

Help students understand how the amount of force varies.

Sport activities usually demand controlled force rather than doing something "as hard as possible."

Game Activity

Firefighter

Supplies: None
Skill: Running

A fire chief runs around the outside of a circle of children and taps a number of them on the back, saying "Firefighter" each time. After making the round of the circle, the chief goes to the center. When she says "Fire," the firefighters run counterclockwise around the circle and back to place. The one who returns first and is able to stand in place motionless is declared the winner and the new chief.

The chief can use other words to fool children, but they run only on the word Fire. This merely provides some fun, since there is no penalty for a false start. The circle children can sound the siren as the firefighters run.

Animal Tag

Supplies: None
Skills: Imagery, running, dodging

Two parallel lines are drawn about 40 ft apart. Children are divided into two groups, each of which takes a position on one of the lines. Children in one group get together with their leader and decide what animal they wish to imitate. Having selected the animal, they move over to within 5 ft or so of the other line. There they imitate the animal, and the other group tries to guess the animal correctly. If the guess is correct, they chase the first group back to its line, trying to tag as many as possible. Those caught must go over to the other team. The second group then selects an animal, and the roles are reversed. If the guessing team cannot guess the animal, however, the performing team gets another try. To avoid confusion, children must raise their hands to take turns at naming the animal. Otherwise, many false chases will occur. If children have trouble guessing, the leader of the performing team can give the initial of the animal.

Sneak Attack

Supplies: None
Skills: Marching, running

Two parallel lines are drawn about 60 ft apart. Children are divided into two teams. One team takes a position on one of the lines, with their backs to the area. These are the chasers. The other team is on the other line, facing the area. This is the sneak team. The sneak team moves forward on signal, moving toward the chasers. When they get reasonably close, a whistle or some other signal is given, and the sneak team turns and runs back to their line, chased by the other team. Anyone caught before reaching the line changes to the chase team. The game is repeated, with the roles exchanged.

Lesson Plans for Grades K-2 - Week 11
Individual Rope Jumping Skills

Objectives:
To perform locomotor movements over a rope
To perform fitness development activities
To jump a self-turning rope
To identify body changes during jump roping activities

Equipment Required:
One jump rope for each student
Four cones and signs for four corners
fitness
10 beanbags

Instructional Activities	Teaching Hints

Introductory Activity -- Locomotor Movements with Equipment

Each student is given a jump rope and moves around the area using various basic locomotor movements. On signal, they drop the rope, and jump, hop, or leap over as many ropes as possible.

Any piece of equipment can be used.

If desired, students can turn and jump the rope.

Fitness Development Activity -- Four-Corners Fitness

Outline a large rectangle with a cone at each corner. Place signs with movement tasks on both sides of the cones. Youngsters move around the outside of the rectangle and change movements as they pass each sign. The following movement activities are suggested:

Corner 1. Skipping/Jumping/Hopping
Corner 2. Sliding/Galloping
Corner 3. Various animal movements
Corner 4. Sport imitation movements

Stop the class after 30 seconds of movement and perform fitness challenges. (See text, p. 163-167 for descriptions of challenges.)

Tape alternating segments of silence and music to signal duration of exercise. Music segments (30 seconds) indicate four corner aerobic activity while intervals of silence (45 seconds) announce performance of flexibility and strength development activities.

Allow students to select a fitness challenge they feel capable of performing. This implies that not all youngsters are required to do the same workload. Children differ and their ability to perform fitness workloads differs. Make fitness a personal challenge.

Lesson Focus -- Individual Rope Jumping Skill

The following are lead-up activities for beginning jumpers:
1. Clap hands to a tom-tom beat.
2. Jump in place to a beat without rope. Jump back and forth over rope on floor.
3. Hold both ends of the jump rope in one hand and turn it so a steady rhythm can be made through a consistent turn. Just before the rope hits the ground, the student should practice jumping.
4. Count the rhythm out loud to cue students when to jump.
5. Start jumping the rope one turn at a time--gradually increase the number of turns.
6. Try jogging and jumping rope. The even rhythm of running often makes it easier for some youngsters to jump the rope.

Introduce the two basic jumps:
1. Slow time. Jump twice each time the rope turns. One of the jumps is performed when the rope is overhead and serves as a preparatory jump.
2. Fast time. One jump each time the rope makes a complete turn. No preparatory jump is allowed.

Since rope is a physically taxing activity, it is suggested that time be allowed for recovery. One way to do this is to play less active games such as Ball Passing or Hot Potato (Lesson plans, p. 17) between bouts of rope jumping.

Background music with a strong beat can be motivating for youngsters.

Rope jumping is difficult to master. Be patient and understand that it may take some students a year or two to learn the activity.

Another way to rest students is to have them make shapes, letter, and names with their rope. Tail tag (fold the rope and place it in the waistband) requires trying to pull out the tail of others.

Tommy Tucker's Land

Supplies: About ten beanbags for each game

Skills: Dodging, running

One child, Tommy or Tammi Tucker, stands in the center of a 15-ft square, within which the beanbags are scattered. Tommy is guarding his land and the treasure. The other children chant,

I'm on Tommy Tucker's land,

Picking up gold and silver.

Children attempt to pick up as much of the treasure as they can while avoiding being tagged by Tommy. Any child who is tagged must return the treasure and retire from the game. The game is over when only one child is left or when all of the beanbags have been successfully filched. The teacher may wish to call a halt to the game earlier if a stalemate is reached. In this case, the child with the most treasure becomes the new Tommy.

Variation: This game can be played with a restraining line instead of a square, but there must be boundaries that limit movement.

Change Sides

Supplies: None

Skill: Body management

Two parallel lines are established 30 ft apart. Half of the children are on each line. On signal, all cross to the other line, face the center, and stand at attention. The first group to do this correctly wins a point. Children must be cautioned to use care when passing through the opposite group. They should be spaced well along each line; this allows room for them to move through each group. The locomotor movements should be varied. The teacher may say, "Ready--walk!" Skipping, hopping, long steps, sliding, and other forms of locomotion can be specified. The position to be assumed at the finish can be varied also.

Variation: The competition can be by squads, with two squads on each line.

Lesson Plans for Grades K-2 - Week 12
Movement Skills and Concepts (3)
Running, Racquet Skills, Moving in Different Ways

Objectives:
To recognize variety within locomotor movements
To work independently at circuit training stations
To understand movement concepts of over and under/different ways of moving
To handle a racquet and ball

Equipment Required:
Circuit training signs and cones
One racquets and ball for each child
Hoops (4-6)
8" foam balls (5-7)

Instructional Activities	Teaching Hints

Introductory Activity -- Movement Varieties

Move using a basic locomotor movement (i.e., walking, jumping, hopping, skipping, galloping). Then add variety to the movement by asking students to respond to the following factors:
1. Level--low, high, in between.
2. Direction--straight, zigzag, circular, curved, forward, backward, upward, downward.
3. Size--large, tiny, medium movements.
4. Patterns--forming squares, diamonds, triangles, circles, figure-eights.
5. Speed--slow, fast, accelerate.

Use scatter formation.

Emphasize and reinforce creative responses.

Explain concepts of level, direction, size, and speed. Short explanations laced with activity allow students time to recover.

Fitness Development Activity --Circuit Training

Make signs, put them on cones and place around the perimeter of the teaching area. Students perform the exercise specified at each station while the music is playing.
1. Tortoise and Hare
2. Curl-up variations
3. Hula Hooping on arms
4. Standing Hip Bend
5. Agility run--run back and forth between two designated lines
6. Push-up variations
7. Crab Walk
8. Bend and Twist

Tape alternating segments of silence and music to signal duration of exercise. Music segments (begin at 30 seconds) indicate activity at each station while intervals of silence (10 seconds) announce it is time to stop and move forward to the next station.

Place an equal number of students at each station.

See text, p. 174-186 for descriptions of exercises.

Lesson Focus – Movement Skills and Concepts (3)

Fundamental Skill: Running
1. Run lightly around the area; stop on signal.
2. Run lightly and change directions on signal.
3. Run, turn around with running steps on signal and continue in a new direction.
4. Pick a spot away from you. Run to it and return without bumping anyone.
5. Run low, gradually increase the height. Reverse.
6. Run patterns. Run inside and around objects.
7. Run with high knee action. Add a knee slap with the hand as you run.
8. Run with different steps—tiny, long, light, heavy, criss-cross, wide and others.
9. Run with arms in different positions--circling, overhead, stiff at sides and others (choice).
10. Free running. Concentrate on good knee lift.
11. Run at different speeds.
12. Touch the ground at times with either hand as you run.
13. Run backwards, sideways.
14. Run with exaggerated arm movements and/or high bounce.
15. Practice running, crossing from one line to another.
    a. Cross your feet as you run.
    b. Touch the ground with one and both hands as you run.
    c. Run forward, looking backward over your right shoulder.

Select a few activities from each of the categories so students receive a variety of skills to practice. When possible, integrate the manipulative skill activities with fundamental skill activities. A common error is to teach all the activities from one category. The reason for multiple groups of activities is to provide variety and enhance motivation.

Encourage running under control. Falling down or collisions should be discouraged. Reinforce students who do run under control.

d. Same, but look over the left shoulder.
e. Change direction every few steps.
f. Run to the center, stop completely, then continue.
g. Make two stops going across--first with the right side forward and then with the left side forward as you stop.
h. Run forward and stop. Come back three steps and stop. Continue in forward direction.
i. Do a two-count stop on the way.
j. Run sideways across, leading with one side. Next time lead with the other.
k. Run forward halfway and then backward the rest.
l. Run backward halfway and then forward the rest.
m. Make a full turn in the center and continue. Do this right and left.
n. Provide for student choice.

Use instructional cues:

"Look ahead when running"

"Bend the arms at the elbows and gently move them back and forth"

When teaching running skills, couple them with stopping skills. Encourage effective stopping by bending the knees and lowering the center of gravity.

Manipulative Activity--Paddles and Balls
Individual Activity
1. Place the ball on the paddle face. Roll it around the face.
2. Hit the ball into the air with the paddle. Retrieve and repeat.
3 Bounce the ball into the air, using the paddle, specify number.
4 Bounce the ball into the air, decreasing the height of the bounce until it rests on the face of the paddle.
5 Bounce the ball on the floor.
6 Alternate bouncing upward and to the floor.
7 Dribble the ball and move while dribbling.
8 Choice activity.

Other pieces of manipulative equipment can be used if paddles and balls are not available.

Place the paddles and balls around the perimeter of the area. On signal, students move and pick up a paddle and ball and begin rolling it around the face of the paddle.

Partner Activity
1. One partner tosses the other hits it back.
2. Try batting it back and forth. If using a tennis ball, let it bounce between hits.
3. Place ball on floor and roll it back and forth.

Partners should be close to each other so control of the ball is maintained.

Movement Concept: Over and Under
1. One partner is an obstacle and the other goes over, under, and around the "obstacle." Reverse positions.
2. Copying action. One partner takes a position and the other goes over and under the first. Reverse positions, but try to copy the same sequence.
3. Progressive sequencing. The first child does a movement (over, under, or around). The second child repeats the movement and adds another. The first child repeats the first two movements and adds a third. The second child repeats and adds a forth.

The goal is to **not** touch the partner who is the obstacle.

Encourage creativity and reinforce new ideas.

Movement Concept: Moving in Different Ways
1. Show me different ways to move when your body is in the air part of the time; when your body is always in contact with the floor.
2. Show me different ways you can progress along the floor without using your hands or feet. Can you "walk" using your seat?
3. What are the different ways you can roll and move?
4. What ways can you move sideways? How can you move on all fours?
5. Move across the floor halfway with one movement and the other half with a decidedly different movement.
6. Explore the different ways you can move when leading with selected parts of the body.

Use student demonstration to encourage variety and creativity. Discuss the many ways of solving a movement problem.

Rollee Pollee

Supplies: Many 8" foam balls

Skills: Ball rolling, dodging

Half of the children form a circle; the other half are in the center. Balls are given to the circle players. The circle players roll the balls at the feet and shoes of the center players, trying to hit them. The center players move around to avoid the balls. A center player who is hit leaves the center and joins the circle.

After a period of time or when all of the children have been hit, the teams trade places. If a specified time limit is used, the team having the fewer players hit wins, or the team that puts out all of the opponents in the shorter time wins. Teaching suggestion: The instructor can have the children practice rolling a ball first. Balls that stop in the center are dead and must be taken back to the circle before being put into play again. The preferable procedure is to have the player who recovers a ball roll it to a teammate rather than return to place

Mix and Match

Supplies: None

Skills: Fundamental locomotor movements

A line is established through the middle of the area. Half of the children are on one side and half are on the other. There must be an odd person, the teacher or another child. The teacher gives a signal for children to move as directed on their side of the line. They can be told to run, hop, skip, or whatever. At another signal, children run to the dividing line, and each reaches across to join hands with a child from the opposite group. The goal is to not be left out. Children may reach over but may not cross the line. The person left out is moved to the opposite side so that players left out come from alternating sides of the area.

Variation: The game also can be done with music or a drumbeat, with the players rushing to the centerline to find partners when the rhythm stops.

Lesson Plans for Grades K-2 - Week 13
Rhythmic Movement (Lesson 2)

Objectives:
To be able to lead other students in simple locomotor movements
To move rhythmically
To learn new exercises utilizing a jump rope

Equipment Required:
One jump rope for each student
Plastic gallon jugs and 8" foam rubber balls

Instructional Activities	Teaching Hints

Introductory Activity -- New Leader Warm-Up

Place students in small groups (3-4). Groups move single file around the area, following a leader in the group. On signal, the last person moves to the head of the squad and become the leader. Various types of locomotor movements and/or exercises can be used by leaders to offer variety and challenge.

If students have trouble working small groups, teach the concept of leading and following by working with a partner.

Encourage variety of response.

Fitness Development Activity --Jump Rope Exercises

1. Jump rope - 45 seconds. If not able to jump, practice swinging the rope to the side while jumping
2. Place the rope on the floor and perform locomotor movements around and over the rope. Make different shapes and letters with the rope.
3. Hold the folded rope overhead. Sway from side to side. Twist right and left.
4. Jump rope - 45 seconds.
5. Lie on back with rope held with outstretched arms toward ceiling. Bring up one leg at a time and touch the rope with toes. Lift both legs together. Sit up and try to hook the rope over the feet. Release and repeat.
6. Touch toes with the folded rope.
7. Jump rope - 45 seconds.
8. Place rope on the floor and do various Animal Walks along or over the rope.
9. Do Push-up variations with the rope folded and held between the hands.
10. Jump rope - 45 seconds.

Tape alternating segments (45 seconds in length) of silence and music to signal duration of exercise. Music segments indicate aerobic activity with the jump ropes while intervals of silence announce using the jump ropes to enhance flexibility and strength development.

Space youngsters so they don't hit others with their rope.

Don't worry about non-jumpers. They will learn sooner or later. Give encouragement and keep them motivated.

Lesson Focus—Rhythmic Movement (2)

Rhythmic Activities

Make dances easy for students to learn by implementing some of the following techniques:
1. Teach the dances without using partners.
2. Allow youngsters to move in any direction without left-right orientation.
3. Use scattered formation instead of circles.
4. Emphasize strong movements such as clapping and stamping to increase involvement.
5. Play the music at a slower speed when first learning the dance.
Rhythms should be taught like other sport skills. Avoid striving for perfection so students know it is acceptable to make mistakes. Teach a variety of dances rather than one or two in depth in case some students find it difficult to master a specific dance. Records can be ordered from Wagon Wheel Records, 17191 Corbina Lane #203, Huntington Beach, CA (714) 846-8169.

Carrousel (Swedish)

Records: LS E-13; MAV 1041
Formation: Double circle, facing center. The inner circle, representing a merry-go-round, joins hands. The outer players, representing the riders, place their hands on the hips of the partner in front.
Directions:

Measures	Verse Action
1--16	Moving to the left, children take 12 slow draw steps and stamp on the last three steps. (Step, together, 2, 3, . . . 12, stamp, stamp, stamp, rest)

Measures	Chorus Action
17--24	Moving left, speed up the draw step until it becomes a slide or gallop. Sing the chorus. (Slide, 2, 3, . . . 8)
25--32	Repeat measures 17--24 while moving to the right. (Slide, 2, 3, . . . 8)

During the chorus, the tempo is increased, and the movement is changed to a slide. Children should take short, light slides to prevent the circle from moving out of control.

Variation:
The dance can be done with youngsters holding the perimeter of a parachute.

Jolly Is the Miller (American)

Records: LS E-10; RPT 317

Formation: Double circle, partners facing counterclockwise, As on the inside, with inside hands joined. A Miller is in the center of the circle

Directions:
All sing. Youngsters march counterclockwise, with inside hands joined. During the second line when "the wheel goes round," the dancers turn their outside arm in a circle to form a wheel. Children change partners at the words "right steps forward and the left steps back." The Miller then has a chance to get a partner. The child left without a partner becomes the next Miller.

Hokey Pokey (American)

Records: CAP 6026; MAC 6995; LS E-25

Formation: Single circle, facing center

Directions:
During the first four lines, the children act out the words. During lines 5 and 6, they hold their hands overhead with palms forward and do a kind of hula while turning around in place. During line 7, they stand in place and clap their hands three times. The basic verse is repeated by substituting, successively, the left foot, right arm, left arm, right elbow, left elbow, head, right hip, left hip, whole self, and backside.

Teaching suggestions:
Encourage the youngsters to make large and vigorous motions during the hokey pokey portions and during the turn around. This adds to the fun. The records all feature singing calls, but the action sequence of the different records varies. The children should sing lightly as they follow the directions given on the record.

Chimes of Dunkirk, Var. 1 (French-Belgian)

Records: LS E-7, E-21; HLP-4026; MAV 1042

Formation: Double circle, partners facing

Directions:

Measures	Action
1--2	Stamp three times in place, right-left-right. (Stamp, 2, 3)
3--4	Clap hands three times above the head (chimes in the steeple). (Clap, 2, 3)
5--8	Partner A places both hands on partner B's hips; B places both hands on A's shoulders. Taking four steps, they turn around in place. (Turn, 2, 3, 4) On the next four counts, partner B (on the outside) moves one person to the left with four steps. (Change, 2, 3, 4) Repeat the sequence from the beginning.

Game Activity

Hill Dill

Supplies: None

Skills: Running, dodging

Two parallel lines are established 50 ft apart. One player is chosen to be it and stands in the center between the lines. The other children stand on one of the parallel lines. The center player calls,

Hill Dill! Come over the hill,

Or else I'll catch you standing still!

Children run across the open space to the other line, while the one in the center tries to tag them. Anyone caught helps the tagger in the center. The first child caught is it for the next game. Once children cross over to the other line, they must await the next call.

Bottle Kick Ball

Supplies: Plastic gallon jugs and 8-in. foam balls

Skills: Kicking, trapping

Players form a large circle around 10 to 12 plastic gallon jugs (bowling pins) standing in the middle of the circle. Students kick the balls and try to knock over the bottles.

Variation: Use as many foam balls as necessary to keep all children active. If the group is large, make more than one circle of players.

Lesson Plans for Grades K-2 - Week 14
Throwing Skills (Lesson 1)

Objectives:
To throw a ball using the overhand technique
To throw with velocity using side orientation and opposition
To learn the basic rules of simple game activities

Equipment Required:
Beanbags or fleece balls
Yarnballs
Rag balls or tennis balls
Hoops and/or mats for targets
Music and tape for astronaut drills

Instructional Activities	Teaching Hints
Introductory Activity -- Group Over and Under	
One-half of the class is scattered and is in a curled position. The other half of the class leaps or jumps over the down children. On signal, reverse the groups quickly. In place of a curl, the down children can bridge and the others go under. The down children can also alternate between curl and bridge, as well as move around the area while in bridge position.	Remind students not to touch the students who are in bridge or curl position. Use different locomotor movements.

Instructional Activities	Teaching Hints
Fitness Development Activity -- Astronaut Drills	
1. Walk.	Tape alternating segments of silence and music to signal duration of exercise.
2. Walk on tiptoes while reaching for the sky.	Music segments (30 seconds in duration)
3. Walk with giant strides.	indicate locomotor activities while
4. Freeze; perform various stretches.	intervals of silence (30 seconds)
5. Do a Puppy Dog Walk.	announce freezing and performing
6. Jump like a pogo stick.	flexibility and strength development
7. Freeze; perform Push-up variations.	activities.
8. Walk and swing arms like a helicopter.	
9. Trot lightly and silently.	
10. Slide like and athlete.	Encourage students to place weight on
11. Freeze; perform Curl-up variations.	their arms and shoulder when they are
12. Crab Walk.	moving on all fours.
13. Skip	
14. Freeze; perform trunk development challenges.	Encourage students to select exercise
15. Walk and cool down.	variations they can perform successfully.

Instructional Activities	Teaching Hints
Lesson Focus --Throwing Skills (1)	
Mimetics	Stand sideways to the target with the
1. "Pretend you:	non-throwing side facing the target.
a. have to throw a rock across a big river!"	Emphasize lifting the throwing arm and
b. want to throw a ball over a very tall building!"	pointing at the target with the non-
c. are a javelin thrower and you want to make the longest throw ever!"	throwing arm.
d. are a baseball pitcher and you are throwing a fast ball!"	
Individual Activities	
1. Throw beanbag or fleece ball against the wall. Concentrate on the following points:	Use instructional cues:
a. Feet together	"Raise your elbow to shoulder level."
b. Foot opposite the throwing arm forward	
c. Start with non-throwing side toward the target area	"Start with your non-throwing side to the
2. Throw from one side of the gym and try to hit the other wall.	wall."
Mimetics	"Reach up with your throwing arm like
1. The teacher should cue students and model a good throw.	you are going to pick an apple"
a. Teacher should use terms such as "turn your non-throwing side to the target," "wind-up," "step toward the target," "follow through."	
b. Teacher can also use this time to observe and coach.	"Take a step toward the target when you
c. *Encourage* students to throw *hard*.	throw."

Individual Activities

1. Throwing yarn balls
   a. Throw against a wall or fence. Throw five balls, retrieve, and repeat.
   b. Teach the proper grip.
2. Throw rag balls or tennis balls against cardboard boxes near a wall or fence.
   a. Throw from 20-25 feet depending on skill level. Student should be able to hit the wall.
   b. Retrieve after all the balls have been thrown.
3. Throw at hoops leaning against a wall or fence.
   Throw from a distance so that children can hit the wall, but only with a forceful throw.

Focus on throwing form rather than accuracy.

Emphasize throwing hard! Proper form can only be learned when students try to throw as hard as possible.

Cue students to move their throwing hand behind their head before the throw.

Give each student 4 or 5 balls to throw. They can be placed in a frisbee to keep them from rolling around. When all balls have been thrown, students (on signal) retrieve the same number of balls they have thrown.

Game Activity

Aviator

Supplies: None

Skills: Running, locomotor movements, stopping

Players are parked (in push-up position) at one end of the playing area. The air traffic controller (ATC) is in front of the players and calls out, "Aviators aviators, take off!" Youngsters take off and move like airplanes to the opposite side of the area. The first person to move to the other side and land the plane (get into push-up position facing the ATC) is declared the new ATC.

If the ATC yells out some type of stormy weather, all planes must return to the starting line and resume the parked position. Examples of stormy weather commands are lightning, thunder, hurricane, and tornado. Each ATC is allowed to give stormy weather warnings once.

Sneak Attack

Supplies: None

Skills: Marching, running

Two parallel lines are drawn about 60 ft apart. Children are divided into two teams. One team takes a position on one of the lines, with their backs to the area. These are the chasers. The other team is on the other line, facing the area. This is the sneak team. The sneak team moves forward on signal, moving toward the chasers. When they get reasonably close, a whistle or some other signal is given, and the sneak team turns and runs back to their line, chased by the other team. Anyone caught before reaching the line changes to the chase team. The game is repeated, with the roles exchanged.

Lesson Plans for Grades K-2 - Week 15
Tumbling, Stunts, and Animal Movements (1)

Objectives:
To be able to perform animal walks
To balance body weight in a variety of positions
To be able to manage body weight in tumbling activities

Equipment Required:
Tumbling Mats
8" foam rubber balls (6-8)
Cones

Instructional Activities	Teaching Hints

Introductory Activity – Countdown

Standing with arms stretched overhead, students begin a countdown (10, 9, 8, 7, etc.) and gradually lower themselves into a crouched position with each count. On the words "blast off," they jump upwards and run in different directions. Students can run to a wall and return to their position. After students learn the activity, allow one of them to say, "Blast Off!"

Vary with challenges such as:
1. Different locomotor movements.
2. Various animal walks.
3. Change intervals of counting--slow, fast.

Fitness Development Activity --Animal Movements and Fitness Challenges

1. Puppy Dog Walk--30 seconds.
2. Freeze; perform stretching activities.
3. Lion Walk--30 seconds
4. Freeze; perform abdominal development challenges.
5. Seal Crawl--30 seconds.
6. Freeze; perform push-up position challenges.
7. Elephant Walk--30 seconds.
8. Injured Coyote Walk--30 seconds.
9. Freeze; perform abdominal challenges.
10. Crab Walk—30 seconds.
11. Rabbit Jump—30 seconds

Tape alternating segments (30 seconds in length) of silence and music to signal duration of exercise. Music segments indicate performing animal movements while intervals of silence announce doing the fitness challenges.

A variation is to place animal movement signs throughout the area and instruct students to move from sign to sign performing the appropriate animal movement each time they reach a new sign.

Lesson Focus -- Tumbling, Stunts, and Animal Movements (1)

Animal Movements

Alligator Crawl

Lie facedown on the floor with elbows bent. Move along the floor in alligator fashion, keeping the hands close to the body and the feet pointed out. First, use unilateral movements---that is, right arm and leg moving together---then change to cross-lateral movements.

Kangaroo Jump

Carry the arms close to the chest with the palms facing forward. Place a beanbag or ball between the knees. Move in different directions by taking small jumps without dropping the object.

Puppy Dog Run

Place the hands on the floor, bending the arms and legs slightly. Walk and run like a happy puppy. Look straight ahead. Keeping the head up, in good position, strengthens the neck muscles. Go sideward, backward, and so on. Turn around in place.

Tumbling and Inverted Balances

Rolling Log

Lie on the back with arms stretched overhead. Roll sideways the length of the mat. The next time, roll with the hands pointed toward the other side of the mat. To roll in a straight line, keep the feet slightly apart.

Five groups of activities in this lesson ensure that youngsters receive a variety of experiences. Pick a few activities from each group and teach them alternately. For example, teach one or two animal movements, then a tumbling and inverted balance, followed by a balance stunt, etc. Give equal time to each group of activities

Variations of the Puppy Dog Run
Cat Walk. Use the same position to imitate a cat. Walk softly. Stretch at times like a cat. Be smooth and deliberate.
Monkey Run. Turn the hands and feet so that the fingers and toes point in (toward each other).

Place tumbling mats in the area so all youngsters are in view.

Side Roll

Start on the hands and knees, with one side toward the direction of the roll. Drop the shoulder, tuck both the elbow and the knee under, and roll over completely, returning to the hands-and-knees position. Momentum is needed to return to the original position. Practice rolling back and forth from one hand-and-knee position to another.

Forward Roll

Stand facing forward, with the feet apart. Squat and place the hands on the mat, shoulder width apart, with elbows against the insides of the thighs. Tuck the chin to the chest and make a rounded back. A push-off with the hands and feet provides the force for the roll. Carry the weight on the hands, with the elbows bearing the weight of the thighs. If the elbows are kept against the thighs and the weight is assumed there, the force of the roll is transferred easily to the rounded back. Try to roll forward to the feet. Later, try with the knees together and no weight on the elbows.

Balance Stunts

One-Leg Balance

Lift one leg from the floor. Later, bring the knee up. The arms should be free at first and then assume specified positions: folded across the chest, on the hips, on the head, or behind the back.

Double-Knee Balance

Kneel on both knees, with the feet pointed to the rear. Lift the feet from the ground and balance on the knees. Vary the position of the arms. Experiment with different arm positions.

Head Touch

On a mat, kneel on both knees, with feet pointed backward and arms outstretched backward for balance. Lean forward slowly and touch the forehead to the mat. Recover to position. Vary the arm position.

Individual Stunts

Directional Walk

For a left movement, begin in standing position. Do all of the following simultaneously: Take a step to the left, raise the left arm and point left, turn the head to the left, and state crisply "Left." Close with the right foot back to standing position. Take several steps left and then reverse.

Line Walking

Use a line on the floor, a chalked line, or a board. Walk forward and backward on the line as follows. First, take regular steps. Next, try follow steps---the front foot moving forward and the back foot moving up. The same foot always leads. Then do heel-and-toe steps, bringing the back toe up against the front heel on each step. Finally, hop along the line on one foot. Change to the other foot. The eyes should be focused ahead.

Fluttering Leaf

Keeping the feet in place and the body relaxed, flutter to the ground slowly, just as a leaf would do in autumn. Swing the arms back and forth loosely to accentuate the fluttering.

Elevator

With the arms out level at the sides, pretend to be an elevator going down. Lower the body a little at a time by bending the knees, but keep the upper body erect and the eyes forward. Return to position. Add a body twist to the downward movement. (A drum can be used.)

Don't force students to perform tumbling and inverted balances. If youngsters are fearful, gentle encouragement should be used.

The forward roll demands enough arm strength to keep the head off the mat. If youngsters lack strength, substitute the side roll for the forward roll.

Spotting the forward roll should rarely be used. If many children need to be spotted, the activity is probably too advanced. To spot the forward roll, the spotter should kneel alongside the child and place one hand on the back of the child's head and the other under the thigh. As the child moves through the roll, give an upward lift on the back of the neck to assure the neck does not absorb the weight of the body. This technique should be used for all forward roll variations.

Overweight children are at greater risk in stunts and tumbling activities. Allow them to avoid the tumbling activities if they so choose.

The Directional Walk is designed to aid in establishing right-left concepts. Definite and forceful simultaneous movements of the arm, head (turn), and leg (step) coupled with a crisp enunciation of the direction are the ingredients of this stunt.

Individual stunts are enjoyable challenges that all children can do. Place emphasis on form and balance.

Cross-Legged Stand

Sit with the legs crossed and the body bent partially forward. Respond appropriately to these six commands.

"Touch the right foot with the right hand."
"Touch the left foot with the right hand."
"Touch the right foot with the left hand."
"Touch the left foot with the left hand."
"Touch both feet with the hands."
"Touch the feet with crossed hands."

The commands should be given in varied sequences. The child must interpret that his right foot is on the left side, and vice versa. If this seems too difficult, have children start with the feet in normal position (uncrossed).

Variation: Do the stunt with a partner, one child giving the commands and the other responding as directed.

Partner and Group Stunts

Bouncing Ball

Toss a lively utility ball into the air and watch how it bounces lower and lower until it finally comes to rest on the floor. From a bent-knee position with the upper body erect, imitate the ball by beginning with a high bounce and gradually lowering the height of the jump to simulate the ball coming to rest. Children should push off from the floor with the hands to gain additional height and should absorb part of the body weight with their hands as well. Toss a real ball into the air and move with the ball.

Try this with a partner, one partner serving as the bouncer and the other as the ball. Reverse positions. Try having one partner dribble the ball in various positions.

Seesaw

Face and join hands with a partner. Move the seesaw up and down, one child stooping while the other rises. Recite the words to this version of "Seesaw, Margery Daw."

Seesaw, Margery Daw,
Maw and Paw, like a saw,
Seesaw, Margery Daw.

Variation: Jump upward at the end of the rise each time.

Game Activity

Circle Straddle Ball

Supplies: Two or more 8-in. foam balls
Skills: Ball rolling, catching

Children are in circle formation, facing in. Each stands in a wide straddle stance with the side of the foot against the neighbor's. The hands are on the knees. Two balls are used. The object of the game is to roll one of the balls between the legs of another player before he can get his hands down to stop the ball. Each time a ball goes between the legs of an individual, a point is scored. The players having the fewest points scored against them are the winners. Keep the circles small so students have more opportunities to handle the ball.

Teaching suggestion: The teacher should be sure that children catch and roll the ball, rather than batting it. Children must keep their hands on their knees until a ball is rolled at them. After some practice, the following variation can be played.

Variation: One child is in the center with a ball and is it. The other children are in the same formation as before. One ball is used. The center player tries to roll the ball through the legs of any child. She should mask her intent, using feints and changes of direction. Any child allowing the ball to go through his legs becomes it.

Statues

Supplies: None
Skills: Body management, applying force, balance

Children are scattered in pairs around the area. One partner is the swinger and the other the statue. The teacher voices a directive, such as "Pretty," "Funny," "Happy," "Angry," or "Ugly." The swinger takes the statue by one or both hands, swings it around in a small circle two or three times (the teacher should specify), and releases it. The statue then takes a pose in keeping with the directive, and the swinger sits down on the floor.

The teacher or a committee of children can determine which children are the best statues. The statue must hold the position without moving or be disqualified. After the winners are announced, the partners reverse positions. Children should be cautioned that the purpose of the swinging is to position the statues and that it must be controlled.

Variation: In the original game, the swinging is done until the directive is called. The swinger then immediately releases the statue, who takes the pose as called. This gives little time for the statue to react. Better and more creative statues are possible if the directive is given earlier.

Soap Bubbles

Supplies: Cones to delineate space, music

Skills: Body management

Each player is a soap bubble floating throughout the area. The teacher calls out the locomotor movement youngsters use to move in the area. The entire area is used to start the game. As the game progresses, the size of the area is decreased by moving the cones. Bubbles freeze on signal. Music can be used to stimulate movement.

The object of the game is not to touch or collide with another bubble. When this occurs, both bubbles burst and sink to the floor and make themselves as small as possible. The space is made smaller until those who have not been touched are declared the winners. Those players who are broken bubbles may move to the unrestricted area and move.

Lesson Plans for Grades K-2 - Week 16
Manipulative Ball Skills--Basketball Related

Objectives:
To be able to follow simple rules of tag games and demonstrate cooperation skills
To perform basketball related skills including:
    chest and bounce pass
    dribbling
    shooting

Equipment Required:
One 8½" playground ball for each
    student
Hoops
Cardboard boxes for ball shooting
    practice
Wand or yardstick

Instructional Activities	Teaching Hints
Introductory Activity -- Free Activity with Playground (Rubber) Balls	
Allow students to practice ball control skills. Encourage challenge by allowing them move if they are able to control the ball in place. Activities can range from tossing and catching to dribbling.	Place the balls around the perimeter of the area. On signal, students move throughout the area, acquire a ball and practice doing a favorite activity.
Fitness Development Activity --Fitness Games and Challenges	
1. Stoop Tag.	Alternate simple tag games with fitness challenge activities. Exercise all parts of the body including upper body and abdominal strength and flexibility.
2. Freeze; perform stretching activities.	
3. Back-to-Back Tag.	
4. Freeze; perform Abdominal Challenges using Curl-up variations.	
5. Balance Tag.	
6. Freeze; perform Arm-Shoulder Girdle Challenges using Push-up variations.	See text, p. 168-169 for descriptions of fitness games.
7. Elbow Swing Tag.	
8. Freeze; perform Trunk Development challenges.	
9. Color Tag.	Ask students what their favorite tag game is and play it.
Lesson Focus -- Manipulative Ball Skills (Basketball Related)	
1. Warm-up with informal passing back and forth between partners.	Have students get toe to toe with a partner. One partner gets a ball, returns, and starts passing to their partner.
2. Push (chest) pass--two handed. Emphasize one or two of the following points at a time depending on the skill level of students:	
a. Ball at chest level, face partner.	
b. Fingers spread above center of ball.	Reach for the ball when making the catch. As the ball is caught, bend the arms and bring the ball to the body to absorb the force.
c. Step toward partner and extend arms.	
d. Throw to chest level.	
e. Catch with finger tips.	
f. Thumbs together for high pass.	
g. Little fingers together for low pass.	
h. Hands relaxed, provide a little "give."	
i. Add the bounce pass—same technique.	The ball should be bounced slightly pass the midway point nearer the receiver and should bounce to chest level.
3. One-Handed Pass	
a. Side toward catcher.	
b. Ball back with both hands to side of head or above shoulder. Fingers spread, directly behind the ball.	
c. Release the forward hand and throw with a wrist snap.	Foam rubber balls (8") are lighter than playground balls. They are easier to catch and make students more confident and less fearful. Use them if they are available.
d. Practice both right and left.	
4. Birdie in the Cage	
a. Form circles of 7-8 children.	
b. Pass ball among the circle for practice. Be sure everyone handles the ball.	
c. Select "Birdie," put in center until he touches the ball, or there is a loose ball leaving the circle.	
5. Dribbling (each has a ball)	Practice dribbling in place before moving and dribbling.
a. Explain technique: wrist action, finger control, eyes ahead.	
b. Dribble in different directions. Use right and left in turn.	

6. One-Handed Shot
    a. Raise ball up to eye level, sight, and shoot to a partner (demonstrate).
    b. Shoot into cardboard boxes placed around the perimeter of the area
    b. Shoot at lowered baskets with partners alternating shooting and rebounding.
7. Add a short dribble and a shot.

Lower the baskets so students don't have to fling the ball. The important goal in shooting is correct form. Shooting at boxes and garbage cans allows students to use proper shooting "touch."

Game Activity

Blindfolded Duck

Supplies: A wand, broomstick, cane, or yardstick
Skills: Fundamental locomotor movements

One child, designated the duck (Daisy if a girl, Donald if a boy), stands blindfolded in the center of a circle and holds a wand or similar article. She taps on the floor and tells children to hop (or perform some other locomotor movement). Children in the circle act accordingly, all moving in the same direction. Daisy then taps the wand twice on the floor, which signals all children to stop. Daisy moves forward with her wand, still blindfolded, to find a child in the circle. She asks, "Who are you?" The child responds, "Quack, quack." Daisy tries to identify this person. If the guess is correct, the identified child becomes the new duck. If the guess is wrong, Daisy must take another turn. After two unsuccessful turns, another child is chosen to be the duck.

Cat and Mice

Supplies: None
Skills: Running, dodging

Children form a large circle. One child is the cat and four others are the mice. The cat and mice cannot leave the circle. On signal, the cat chases the mice inside the circle. As they are caught, the mice join the circle. The last mouse caught becomes the cat for the next round.
Teaching suggestions: The teacher should start at one point in the circle and go around the circle selecting mice so that each child gets a chance to be in the center.
Sometimes, one child has difficulty catching the last mouse or any of the mice. If this is the case, children forming the circle can take a step toward the center, thus constricting the running area. The teacher should cut off any prolonged chase sequence.

Freeze

Supplies: Music or tom-tom
Skills: Locomotor movements to rhythm

Children are scattered about the room. When the music starts, they move throughout the area, guided by the music. They walk, run, jump, or use other locomotor movements, depending on the selected music or beat. When the music is stopped, they freeze and do not move. Any child caught moving after the cessation of the rhythm pays a penalty. A tom-tom or a piano is a fine accompaniment for this game, because the rhythmic beat can be varied easily and the rhythm can be stopped at any time.

This is an excellent game for practicing management skills. The game reinforces freezing on a stop signal.
Variations:

1. Specify the level at which children must freeze.

2. Have children fall to the ground or balance or go into a different position, such as the Push-Up, Crab, Lame Dog, or some other defined position.

Lesson Plans for Grades K-2 - Week 17
Movement Skills and Concepts (4)
Sliding, Galloping, Tossing and Catching

Objectives

To identify and place body parts on an objects

To work cooperative with others in the parachute activity

To perform a variety of gallop and slide steps

To demonstrate body management skills by performing a variety of movements through hoops

Equipment Required:

One beanbag for each child

One hoop for each child

Parachute

10-12 beanbags or balls for the game

Instructional Activities	Teaching Hints

Introductory Activity -- Body Part Identification

Each student stands near a beanbag placed on the floor. Students are instructed to move over and around the beanbags on the floor. When a body part is called, students place the body part on the nearest beanbag.

Variations:
1. Use different movements.
2. Use different body parts
3. Call combinations of movements and body parts.

Students should be encouraged to move over and around as many beanbags as possible.

Challenge students by calling out a color. They then must avoid moving over and around all beanbags of that color.

Fitness Development Activity --Parachute Fitness

1. Jog while holding the chute in the left hand. (music)
2. Shake the chute. (no music)
3. Slide while holding the chute with both hands. (music)
4. Sit and perform curl-ups. (no music)
5. Skip. (music)
6. Freeze, face the center, and stretch the chute tightly. Hold for 8-12 seconds. Repeat. (no music)
7. Run in place while holding the chute taut at different levels. (music)
8. Sit with legs under the chute. Do a seat walk toward the center. Return to the perimeter. Repeat four to six times. (no music)
9. Place the chute on the ground. Jog away from the chute and return on signal. Repeat. (music)
10. Move into push-up position holding the chute with one hand. Shake the chute. (no music)
11. Shake the chute and jump in place. (music)
12. Lie on back with feet under the chute. Shake the chute with the feet. (no music)
13. Hop to the center of the chute and return. Repeat. (music)
14. Sit with feet under the chute. Stretch by touching the toes with the chute. Relax with other stretches while sitting. (no music)

Tape alternating segments of silence and music to signal duration of exercise. Music segments indicate aerobic activity with the parachute while intervals of silence announce using the chute to enhance flexibility and strength development.

Space youngsters evenly around the chute.

Use different hand grips (palms up, down, mixed).

All movements should be done under control. Some of the faster and stronger students will have to moderate their performance.

Lesson Focus – Movement Skills and Concepts (4)

Fundamental Skill: Sliding
1. Slide in one direction, stop and slide in another.
2. Begin with short slides in crease slide length. Reverse.
3. Do a number of slides (3, 4, 5, 6), do a half turn, continue in the same direction, but leading with the other leg.
4. Slide with a 4-4 pattern.
5. Slide in a figure-eight pattern.
6. Change levels while sliding; touch the floor occasionally while sliding.
7. Slide lightly and noiselessly.
8. Pretend to be a defensive basketball player, sliding.
9. Slide with a partner.

Select a few activities from each of the categories so students receive a variety of skills to practice. When possible, integrate the manipulative skill activities with fundamental skill activities.

Use instructional cues:

"Move sideways"

"Don't cross the feet"

Fundamental Skill: Galloping

1. Form a circle. Slide in one direction (clockwise or counterclockwise). Gradually turn the body to face the line of direction; this is galloping.
2. Practice galloping freely in general space. Gallop backwards.
3. Gallop in a figure-eight and other patterns.
4. Change gallops (leading foot) on 8, 4 and 2 gallops.
5. Gallop with a partner.

Show the relationship between the slide and gallop steps. The gallop is simply a sliding step performed in a forward direction.

Show the uneven rhythm of the gallop.

Manipulative Skills: Hoop Activities

Each group uses four or five hoops and places them in a line on the floor.
1. Walk, hop, and jump through or on the sides of the hoops.
2. Leap over the hoops from the side.
3. Run around the hoops.
4. Jump astride the hoop and inside it alternately.
5. Jump through each center without touching the hoop.
6. Use different animal walks--Bunny Jump, Frog Jump, Crab Walk.
7. Jump down the line of hoops.
8. Using one hoop, take a push-up position. Keeping the hands on the hoop, circle with the feet. Then put the feet on the hoop and circle with the hands.
9. Jog through with high knees.
10. Do heel clicks in the center of each hoop.
11. Roll a hoop at a partner, who jumps over it as it approaches.

This is an excellent activity to teach cooperative skills. Youngsters should be encouraged to design their hoop patterns and to take turns performing through the hoops.

Near the end of the hoop activities, allow students time to pick up a hoop and perform individual activities.

Movement Concept: Movement Combinations

1. Run, leap, roll.
2. Shake (all over), gallop, freeze.
3. Hop, collapse, explode.
4. Whirl, skip, sink (melt) slowly.
5. Creep, pounce, curl.
6. Begin low, lift, grin, roll.
7. Kneel, sway, jump to feet.
8. Shrink, expand, slide.
9. On all fours, run, roll, jump.
10. Do a Jumping Jack (two or three times), slide, jump turn.

Encourage individual response. Use student demonstration to illustrate the breadth of responses.

Offer students the opportunity to demonstrate their response to a partner. Each partner then tries to imitate the other's combination.

Game Activity

Hot Potatoes

Supplies: One to three balls or beanbags for each group

Skill: Object handling

Children are seated in small circles (8 to 12 per circle) so that objects can be passed from one to another around the circle. Balls or beanbags or both are passed around the circle. The teacher or a selected student looks away from the class and randomly shouts, "stop!" The point of the game is to avoid getting stuck with an object. If this happens, the player(s) with an object must get up and move to the next circle. The teacher should begin the game with one object and gradually add objects if the class is capable.

Variation: The passing direction can be reversed on signal.

Popcorn

Supplies: None

Skills: Curling, stretching, jumping

The teacher should give a short preliminary explanation of how popcorn pops in response to the heat applied. Half of the children are designated as popcorn; they crouch down in the center of the circle formed by the rest of the children. The circle children, also crouching, represent the heat. One of them is designated the leader, and his actions serve as a guide to the other children. The circle children gradually rise to a standing position, extend their arms overhead, and shake them vigorously to indicate the intensifying heat. In the meantime, the popcorn in the center starts to pop. This should begin at a slow pace and increase in speed and height as the heat is applied. In the final stages, children are popping up rapidly. After a time, the groups change places and the action is repeated.

Lesson Plans for Grades K-2 - Week 18
Recreational Activities

Objectives:
To be able to move continuously in moderately active activities
To learn the rules of recreational activities
To play in recreational activities independently without adult supervision

Equipment Required:
One hoop or beanbag per student for Ponies in the Stable
Music for astronaut drills
Equipment for desired recreational activities

Instructional Activities	Teaching Hints

Introductory Activity -- Ponies in the Stable

A beanbag or hoop is used to mark each child's stable. On signal, youngsters gallop around the area and in and out of "stables." On a second signal, students return to the nearest stable.
Variations.
1. Use different locomotor movements.
2. Take different positions in the stable such as seated, balanced, collapsed.

To introduce excitement into the activity, remove a few stables and encourage students not to be left out.

Teach directions by asking students to move in a certain direction, i.e., north, south, etc.

Fitness Development Activity --Astronaut Drills

1. Walk.
2. Walk on tiptoes while reaching for the sky.
3. Walk with giant strides.
4. Freeze; perform various stretches.
5. Do a Puppy Dog Walk.
6. Jump like a pogo stick.
7. Freeze; perform Push-up challenges.
8. Walk and swing arms like a helicopter.
9. Trot lightly and silently.
10. Slide like and athlete.
11. Freeze; perform Curl-up challenges.
12. Crab Walk.
13. Skip
14. Freeze; perform trunk development challenges.
15. Walk and cool down.

Tape alternating segments of silence and music to signal duration of exercise. Music segments (30 seconds in duration) indicate locomotor activities while intervals of silence (30 seconds) announce freezing and performing flexibility and strength development activities.

See text, p. 163-167 for descriptions of challenges.

Lesson Focus and Game Activity -- Recreational Activities

The purpose of this unit is to teach children activities that they can use for recreation outside of school or during recess. Suggested activities are:
1. Shuffleboard
2. Two Square
3. Hopscotch
4. Beanbag Horseshoes
5. Jacks
6. Marbles
7. Sidewalk tennis
8. Quoits
9. Rubber Horseshoes
10. Four Square
11. Basketball, Soccer, and other seasonal sports
12. Any traditional and/or local area games

Teach students the rules of recreational activities so they are able to participate effectively during free-time.

Teach any games that are traditional to an area. Older youngsters may be a good source of advice for often-played games.

If desired, set up a number of stations and have youngsters rotate to different stations during the lesson.

Lesson Plans for Grades K-2 - Week 19
Movement Skills and Concepts
Skipping, Catching with Scoops, Leading, and Body Support

Objectives:
To skip and demonstrate a number of skipping variations
To be able to support the body weight with the arms.
To understand the concept of leading
To handle a ball with an implement

Equipment Required:
Cones and signs for four corners
   movement
Scoops and balls

Instructional Activities	Teaching Hints

Introductory Activity -- Following Activity

One partner leads and performs various kinds of movements. The other partner must move in a similar fashion. This can also be used with squads or small groups, allowing the captain to lead.

Student demonstration can be used to stimulate new ideas among students.

Fitness Development Activity --Four Corners Fitness

Outline a large rectangle with a cone at each corner. Place signs with movement tasks on both sides of the cones. Youngsters move around the outside of the rectangle and change movements as they pass each sign. The following movement activities are suggested:

   Corner 1. Skipping/Jumping/Hopping
   Corner 2. Sliding/Galloping
   Corner 3. Various animal movements
   Corner 4. Sport imitation movements

Stop the class after 30 seconds of movement and perform fitness challenges (see Lesson 6, p. 00).

Tape alternating segments of silence and music to signal duration of exercise. Music segments (30 seconds) indicate four corner aerobic activity while intervals of silence (45 seconds) announce performance of flexibility and strength development activities.

Faster moving students should pass on the outside of the area.

If signs are not used at the corners, teachers can specify by voice what movements are to be performed.

Lesson Focus -- Movement Skills and Concepts (5)

Fundamental Skill: Skipping
1. Skip in general space.
2. Vary the skip with exaggerated arm action and lifted knees; side-to-side motion; skip lightly; skip heavily.
3. Skip backward.
4. Clap as you skip.
5. Skip twice on the same side (double skip). Alternate double skips (two on each side).
6. Form a circle. Skip clockwise and counterclockwise.
7. Form by partners or by threes. Skip in general space.

Manipulative Skills: Scoop And Ball Activities
Individual Activities
1. Place the ball on the floor, scoop it up with the scoop.
2. Toss the ball upward and catch it with the scoop. Change scoop to the other hand and repeat.
3. Explore various ways of tossing the ball with the hand and catching in the scoop.
4. Throw the ball against a wall and catch with the scoop.
5. Throw the ball against the wall with the scoop and catch with the scoop.
6. Toss either with the hand or with the scoop and do a stunt before catching. Use heel click, quarter turn, touch scoop to floor.
7. Exploratory opportunity.

Select a few activities from each of the categories so students receive a variety of skills to practice. When possible, integrate the manipulative skill activities with fundamental skill activities. A common error is to teach all the activities from one category. The reason for multiple groups of activities is to provide variety and enhance motivation.

For students having problems with skipping, be patient. To help them learn, slow down the movement to a step and hop on the same foot. Gradually speed it up to a skip.

Empty and washed plastic gallon jugs make excellent scoops. Cut out half of the bottle opposite the hand and a scoop remains.

Partner Activities

1. Roll the ball and pick up with the scoop.
2. Throw the ball back and forth, catching in the scoop.
3. Toss the ball on first bounce and catch in the scoop.
4. Repeat some of the previous activities and toss with the scoop.
5. Explore from other positions--sitting, kneeling, back to back, prone position.

Yarn balls are excellent with scoops when teaching control skill because they do not travel far when missed. Also, students can apply more force to the racquet which helps develop proper form.

Movement Concept: Supporting Body Weight with the Hands

1. Begin in all-fours position, practice taking the weight on the hands by kicking up the feet in a one-two fashion.
2. From standing position with the arms overhead, bring the hands to the floor and take the weight on the hands.
3. Take the weight successively on the hands by moving from the side as a preliminary to the cartwheel.
4. Have a partner hold your knees in a wheelbarrow position. Lift the legs as high as possible. May need to shift hands underneath.

If these activities are too difficult for some children, have them start on all fours and gently kick the feet off the floor.

When using partner activities that are weight bearing, match them so they are similar in weight.

Movement Concept: Leading with Different Body Parts

Children move across the space as indicated:
1. Move across with one arm leading.
2. Now a different movement with the other arm leading.
3. Repeat 1 with one foot leading.
4. Repeat 2 with other fool leading.
5. Move so one arm and one foot are leading.
6. Show us a movement where the shoulder leads.
7. How about a movement where one side leads?
8. Show a movement along the floor where the foot is leading.
9. Can you move so your head leads the movement?
10. What other kinds of leading parts can you show?

Use different locomotor movements.

Use different qualities of movement such as speed or force. Encourage use of general and personal space when moving.

Allow students to develop their personal movement and direction.

Movement Concept: Body Support

1. Make a bridge using five, four, three, and two parts of the body.
2. Select the number of body parts you wish to use and see how many different bridges you can make from this base.
3. Select three different bridges and go from one to the next smoothly in sequence (sustained flow).
4. Work with a partner and make different kinds of bridges.
5. Have your partner go under your bridge.

Bridges are an excellent way to begin learning about supporting body weight.

Emphasize creatively changing from one type of bridge to another.

When working with a partner, avoid touching each other.

Game Activity

Hill Dill

Supplies: None

Skills: Running, dodging

Two parallel lines are established 50 ft apart. One player is chosen to be it and stands in the center between the lines. The other children stand on one of the parallel lines. The center player calls,

Hill Dill! Come over the hill,

Or else I'll catch you standing still!

Children run across the open space to the other line, while the one in the center tries to tag them. Anyone caught helps the tagger in the center. The first child caught is it for the next game. Once children cross over to the other line, they must await the next call.

Mousetrap

Supplies: None

Skills: Skipping, running, dodging

Half of the children form a circle with hands joined and face the center. This is the trap. The other children are on the outside of the circle. These are the mice. Three signals are given for the game. These can be word cues or other signals. On the first signal, the mice skip around, outside the circle, playing happily. On the second signal, the trap is opened. (The circle players raise their joined hands to form arches.) The mice run in and out of the trap. On the third signal, the trap snaps shut. (The arms come down.) All mice caught inside join the circle. The game is repeated until all or most of the mice are caught. The players then exchange places, and the game begins anew. A child should not run in and out of the trap through adjacent openings.

Lesson Plans for Grades K-2 - Week 20
Tumbling, Stunts, and Animal Movements (2)

Objectives:
To sustain moderate physical activity
To absorb the body weight on the hands
To balance the body in a variety of challenges

Equipment Required:
Cones and circuit training signs
Hoops for circuit training
Tumbling mats
Beanbags for Partner Toe Toucher

Instructional Activities	Teaching Hints
Introductory Activity -- Popcorn	
Students pair up with one person on the floor in push-up position and the other standing ready to move. On signal, the standing students move over and under the persons on the floor. The person on the floor changes from a raised to a lowered push-up position each time the partner goes over or under her. On signal, reverse positions.	Caution to avoid touching others and respect personal space. Challenge students to see how many students they can move over and under.

Fitness Development Activity -- Circuit Training

Make signs, put them on cones and place around the perimeter of the teaching area. Students perform the exercise specified at each station while the music is playing.
1. Tortoise and Hare
2. Abdominal challenges
3. Hula Hooping on arms
4. Standing Hip Bend
5. Agility run--run back and forth between two designated lines
6. Push-up challenges
7. Crab Walk
8. Bend and Twist

Tape alternating segments of silence and music to signal duration of exercise. Music segments (begin at 30 seconds) indicate activity at each station while intervals of silence (10 seconds) announce it is time to stop and move forward to the next station.

Encourage youngsters to do their personal best.

See text, p. 174-186 for descriptions of exercises.

Lesson Focus – Tumbling, Stunts, and Animal Movements (2)

Animal Movements

Bear Walk
 Bend forward and touch the ground with both hands. Travel forward slowly by moving the hand and foot on the same side together (i.e., first the right hand and foot, then the left hand and foot). Make deliberate movements.

Gorilla Walk
 Bend the knees and carry the trunk forward. Let the arms hang at the sides. Touch the fingers to the ground while walking.

Rabbit Jump
 Crouch with knees apart and hands placed on the floor. Move forward by reaching out with both hands and then bringing both feet up to the hands. The eyes look ahead. Emphasize that this is a jump rather than a hop because both feet move at once.

Elephant Walk
 Bend well forward, clasping the hands together to form a trunk. The end of the trunk should swing close to the ground. Walk in a slow, deliberate, dignified manner, keeping the legs straight and swinging the trunk from side to side.

Tumbling and Inverted Balances
Forward Roll Review (See Lesson 15)

Five groups of activities in this lesson ensure that youngsters receive a variety of experiences. Pick a few activities from each group and teach them alternately. For example, teach one or two animal movements, then a tumbling and inverted balance, followed by a balance stunt, etc. Give equal time to each group of activities

Scatter tumbling mats throughout the area so that there is little standing in line waiting for a turn.

A major concern for safety is the neck and back region. Overweight children are at greater risk and might be allowed to avoid tumbling and inverted balances.

Do not perform many repetitions of tumbling and inverted balances. For most children, limiting the number of forward or backward roll repetitions to four or five will prevent fatigue and injury.

Backward Curl

Approach this activity in three stages. For the first stage, begin in a sitting position, with the knees drawn up to the chest and the chin tucked. The hands are clasped and placed behind the head with the elbows held out as far as possible. Gently roll backward until the weight is on the elbows. Roll back to starting position.

In stage two, perform the same action as before, but place the hands alongside the head on the mat while rolling back. The fingers are pointed in the direction of the roll, with palms down on the mat. (A good cue is, "Point your thumbs toward your ears and keep your elbows close to your body.")

For stage three, perform the same action as in stage two, but start in a crouched position on the feet with the back facing the direction of the roll. Momentum is secured by sitting down quickly and bringing the knees to the chest. This, like the Back Roller, is a lead-up to the Backward Roll. Teach children to push against the floor to take pressure off the back of the neck.

Climb-Up

Begin on a mat in a kneeling position, with hands placed about shoulder width apart and the fingers spread and pointed forward. Place the head forward of the hands, so that the head and hands form a triangle on the mat. Walk the body weight forward so that most of it rests on the hands and head. Climb the knees to the top of the elbows. (This stunt is a lead-up to the Headstand.)

Balance Stunts

Kimbo Stand

With the left foot kept flat on the ground, cross the right leg over the left to a position in which the right foot is pointed partially down and the toe is touching the ground.

Knee-Lift Stand

From a standing position, lift one knee up so that the thigh is parallel to the ground and the toe is pointed down. Hold. Return to starting position.

Stork Stand

From a standing position, shift all of the weight to one foot. Place the other foot so that the sole is against the inside of the knee and thigh of the standing leg. Hold. Recover to standing position.

Individual Stunts

Rubber Band

Get down in a squat position with the hands and arms clasped around the knees. On the command "Stretch, stretch, stretch," stretch as tall and as wide as possible. On the command "Snap," snap back to original position.

Pumping Up the Balloon

One child, the pumper, is in front of the other children, who are the balloons. The pumper pretends to use a bicycle pump to inflate the balloons. The balloons get larger and larger until the pumper shouts, "Bang," whereupon the balloons collapse to the floor. The pumper should give a "shoosh" sound every time a pumping motion is made.

Rising Sun

Lie on the back. Using the arms for balance only, rise to a standing position. Try with the arms folded over the chest.

Heel Click

Stand with the feet slightly apart, jump up, and click the heels, coming down with the feet apart.

The Backward Curl should be used to learn to roll back and forth. No youngster should be expected to roll over if it is difficult for them. In stunts and tumbling, it is important that the student decide if they are capable and confident enough to try the activity.

The Climb-up should only be performed by youngsters who have sufficient strength to support the body weight. Overweight children will find this to be a difficult activity.

Most children can accomplish balance stunts and this should be an area of accomplishment for all students.

Encourage students to hold the balance position for at least five counts.

An added challenge is to see how long the balance can be held with the eyes closed.

Emphasize a quick snapping back to position. Students can change their starting position as they desire.

Allow many children the chance to be a pumper.

Experiment with different positions of the feet. The feet can be crossed, spread wide, both to one side, and so on.

Try with a quarter turn right and left. Try clapping the hands overhead as the heels are clicked.

This an excellent opportunity to talk about cooperation and moving together. Emphasize form rather than doing it as fast as possible

Partner and Group Stunts

Wring the Dishrag

Face and join hands with a partner. Raise one pair of arms (right for one and left for the other) and turn under, continuing a full turn until back to original position. Try in a reverse direction.

Partner Toe Toucher

Partners lie on their backs with heads near each other and feet in opposite directions. Join arms with partner using a hand-wrist grip, and bring the legs up so that the toes touch partner's toes. Keep high on the shoulders and touch the feet high. Strive to attain the high shoulder position, as this is the point of most difficulty

One child carries a beanbag, a ball, or some other article between the feet, and transfers the object to the partner, who lowers it to the floor.

Game Activity

Where's My Partner?

 Supplies: None

 Skills: Fundamental locomotor movements

Children are in a double circle by couples, with partners facing. The inside circle has one more player than the outside. When the signal is given, the circles skip (or walk, run, hop, or gallop) to the right. This means that they are skipping in opposite directions. On the command "Halt," the circles face each other to find partners. The player left without a partner is in the mush pot (the center area of the circle). When play starts again, this child enters either circle. The circles should be reversed after a time.

Variation: The game can also be played with music or a drumbeat. When the music stops, the players seek partners.

Change Sides

 Supplies: None

 Skill: Body management

Two parallel lines are established 30 ft apart. Half of the children are on each line. On signal, all cross to the other line, face the center, and stand at attention. The first group to do this correctly wins a point. Children must be cautioned to use care when passing through the opposite group. They should be spaced well along each line; this allows room for them to move through each group. The locomotor movements should be varied. The teacher may say, "Ready--walk!" Skipping, hopping, long steps, sliding, and other forms of locomotion can be specified. The position to be assumed at the finish can be varied also.

Teaching suggestion: Because success depends on getting across first, the teacher should watch for shortcutting of the rules and talk this problem over with the children.

Variation: The competition can be by squads, with two squads on each line.

Lesson Plans for Grades K-2 - Week 21
Movement Skills and Concepts (6)
Hopping, Hoop Activities, and Body Shapes

Objectives:
To cooperatively play tag games and maintain body control
To hop continuously while performing a variety of challenges
To be able to recognize different shapes and make them with their body

Equipment Required:
One hoop for each child
10-12 foam rubber balls (8")
Tape for Fitness Challenges

Instructional Activities	Teaching Hints
Introductory Activity -- Tag Games	
Use a tag game youngsters enjoy to offer children immediate activity Some suggestions are: 1. Skunk 2. Stork 3. Stoop 4. Nose and Toe	Teach moving under control. Students should understand that they should seldom run as fast as possible in order to prevent collisions. Use different locomotor movements.

Fitness Development Activity --Fitness Challenges

Alternate locomotor movements with strength and flexibility challenges. Repeat the challenges as necessary.

Locomotor Movement: Walk for 30 seconds.

Flexibility and Trunk Development Challenges
1. Bend in different directions.
2. Stretch slowly and return quickly.
3. Combine bending and stretching movements.
4. Sway back and forth.
5. Twist one body part; add body parts.
6. Make your body move in a large circle.
7. In a sitting position, wave your legs at a friend; make circles with your legs.

Locomotor Movement: Skip for 30 seconds.

Shoulder Girdle Challenges
In a push-up position, do the following challenges:
1. Lift one foot; the other foot.
2. Wave at a friend; wave with the other arm.
3. Scratch your back with one hand; use the other hand.
4. Walk your feet to your hands.
5. Turn over and face the ceiling; shake a leg; Crab Walk.

Locomotor Movement: Jog for 30 seconds.

Abdominal Development
From a supine position:
1. Lift your head and look at your toes.
2. Lift your knees to your chest.
3. Wave your legs at a friend. From a sitting position:
1. Slowly lay down with hands on tummy.
2. Lift legs and touch toes.

Locomotor Movement: Run and leap for 30 seconds.

Teaching Hints (continued):

Tape alternating segments (30 seconds in length) of silence and music to signal duration of exercise. Music segments indicate doing the locomotor movements while intervals of silence announce performing the strength and flexibility challenges

See text, p. 163-167 for descriptions of challenges.

Students select the fitness challenge they feel capable of performing. This implies that not all youngsters are required to do the same workload. Children differ and their ability to perform fitness workloads differs. Make fitness a personal challenge.

Because students can select activities they feel able to do, there is little reason for not trying.

If students do not remember the various challenges, cue them by calling out a number of the activities. They can select one they enjoy.

Use different qualities of movement such as giant skips, quick gallops, tiny jogging steps, etc.

Animal walks can be substituted for locomotor movements.

Lesson Focus -- Movement Skills and Concepts (6)

Fundamental Skill: Hopping

1. Hopping (Hopping is done on one foot only)
   a. Hop in place lightly, changing the feet at will.
   b. Hop numbered sequences, right and left: 1-1, 2-2, 3-3, 4-4, 5-5, 1-2, 2-1, 2-3, 3-2 (hop in place).
   c. Hop, increasing height, reverse.
   d. From your spot, take two, three, or four hops out, turn around and hop back on other foot. How much space can you cover?
   e. Hop on one foot, do a heel and toe pattern with the other. Can you change feet each time doing this?
   f. Pick two spots away from you. Hop in place, then move to one spot. Hop in place, then to the other. Return to spot.
   g. Hop forward, backward, sideways.
   h. Hop different patterns--square, triangle, circle, figure-eight, diamond, etc.
   i. Explore different positions in which you can hold the foot while hopping.
   j. Hold the free foot in different positions while hopping.
   k. Hop with the body in different leaning positions--forward, sideways, backward.
   l. Hop lightly, heavily.
   m. While hopping, touch the floor with either or both hands.
   n. Hop back and forth over a board or line, moving down the line.
   o. Trace out letters or numbers. Write your name hopping.
   p. Do quarter or half turns while hopping.

Manipulative Skills: Floor Targets and Hula Hooping

1. Jump in an out of the hoop.
2. Work with a partner and follow the leader through two hoops.
3. Jump in an out of a hoop held by a friend.
4. Hula hoop around the waist.
5. Hula hoop around the hands and arms, the neck, or legs (on back position).
6. Exploratory activity.

Movement Concept: Body Shapes

Possibilities include: Long or short; wide or narrow; straight or twisted; stretched or curled; large or small.

1. Show me a _____ (use terms above) shape.
2. When I say "change," go from a _____ shape to a _____ shape (vary these).
3. Explore symmetrical and asymmetrical. Take one of the above and make it symmetrical. Then change the same to an asymmetrical shape.
4. Explore other kinds of shapes.
5. Contrasting shapes. Do one kind of shape and its contrast. Or name a shape with its contrast or opposite.

Movement Concept: Letters with the Body

1. Make letters standing.
2. Make letters lying on the floor.
3. Divide class into two sets of groups: one group makes a letter and the other names it. Give only one guess. Change groups.
4. Make simple words of two letters or three letters, using one child per letter.
5. Form numbers of two digits.

Select a few activities from each of the categories so students receive a variety of skills to practice. When possible, integrate the manipulative skill activities with fundamental skill activities. A common error is to teach all the activities from one category. The reason for multiple groups of activities is to provide variety and enhance motivation.

Use instructional cues for hopping such as:

"Stay on your toes."

"Swing your arms upward."

"Use your arms for balance."

Change feet regularly so students learn to hop on both. Also, a little hopping goes a long ways. Children fatigue quickly.

Place the hoops around the perimeter of the area. On signal, students move to acquire a hoop and return performing a specified activity.

Teach what the shapes are like to make sure students know what they are. After they have been learned, start to encourage quick response to the shape commands.

Allow students time to think about the shapes of the letters and numbers.

Printing large letters on cards can help youngsters visualize the desired shape.

Game Activity

Rollee Pollee

Supplies: Many 8" foam balls

Skills: Ball rolling, dodging

Half of the children form a circle; the other half are in the center. Balls are given to the circle players. The circle players roll the balls at the feet and shoes of the center players, trying to hit them. The center players move around to avoid the balls. A center player who is hit leaves the center and joins the circle.

After a period of time or when all of the children have been hit, the teams trade places. If a specified time limit is used, the team having the fewer players hit wins, or the team that puts out all of the opponents in the shorter time wins. Teaching suggestion: The instructor can have the children practice rolling a ball first. Balls that stop in the center are dead and must be taken back to the circle before being put into play again. The preferable procedure is to have the player who recovers a ball roll it to a teammate rather than return to place

Stop Ball

Supplies: A ball

Skills: Tossing, catching

One child, with hands over the eyes, stands in the center of a circle of children. A ball is tossed clockwise or counterclockwise from child to child around the circle. Failing to catch the ball or making a bad toss incurs a penalty. That child must take one long step back and stay out of the game for one turn.

At a time of her own selection, the center player calls, "Stop." The player caught with the ball steps back and stays out for one turn. The center player should be allowed three or four turns and then be changed.

Lesson Plans for Grades K-2 - Week 22
Locomotor Skills Using Long Jump Ropes

Objectives:
To continuously move in moderate activity
To demonstrate body management skills by not touching the ropes
To cooperate in game activities

Equipment Required:
12 long jump ropes
Music tape for astronaut drills

Instructional Activities	Teaching Hints

Introductory Activity -- Run, Stop, and Pivot

Have the children run, and on signal, stop and pivot. Begin teaching a 90° pivot and move gradually to a 180° pivot. Relate the use of the pivot to various sport activities, such as basketball.

Encourage moving under control.

Bend the knees when stopping and place the weight on the pivot foot.

Fitness Development Activity --Astronaut Drills

1. Walk.
2. Walk on tiptoes while reaching for the sky.
3. Walk with giant strides.
4. Freeze; perform various stretches.
5. Do a Puppy Dog Walk.
6. Jump like a pogo stick.
7. Freeze; perform Push-up challenges.
8. Walk and swing arms like a helicopter.
9. Trot lightly and silently.
10. Slide like and athlete.
11. Freeze; perform abdominal challenges.
12. Crab Walk.
13. Skip
14. Freeze; perform trunk development challenges.
15. Walk and cool down.

Tape alternating segments of silence and music to signal duration of exercise. Music segments (30 seconds in duration) indicate locomotor activities while intervals of silence (30 seconds) announce freezing and performing flexibility and strength development activities.

Change direction often to keep children mixed and spread out.

Encourage students to keep moving at their own pace.

Lesson Focus -- Locomotor Skills Using Long Jump Ropes

Single-Rope Activities
1. Jump back and forth, feet uncrossed.
2. Jump back and forth, feet crossed.
3. Jump back and forth, feet crossed and uncrossed alternately.
4. Hop back and forth over rope using right and left feet in turn.
5. Jump the rope and perform various body turns while jumping.
6. Change body shapes and sizes while jumping.
7. Crawl or slide under the rope.
8. Alternate going over and under the rope.
9. Perform crouch jumps back and forth the length of the rope
10. Exploratory activity.

Double Rope Activities
1. Hold the ropes parallel to each other:
   a. Jump in one side and out the other.
   b. Hop in one side and out the other.
   c. Crouch jump in and out of the two ropes.
   d. Perform various animal walks in and out of the ropes.
   e. Allow students to develop personal movements
2. Hold the ropes crossed at right angles to each other.
   a. Perform various movements from one quadrant to the other.
   b. Jump into one quadrant and crawl out the other.
   c. Run from quadrant to quadrant without touching the ropes.

Divide the class into groups of four. This will allow two students to hold the ropes and two to do the activities. Students can switch holding and moving on their own or a signal can be given to change. The ropes should not be moved while students are jumping and moving.

In the beginning phases, the ropes can be laid on the floor and movements practiced by all the students. Also, one end of the rope can be tied to a bench or wall anchor if desired.

Students should approach the rope(s) from one end and progress the length of the jump ropes.

The goal is to not touch the ropes while moving. Also, having the ropes held higher on one end and low at the other will offer increased challenge.

One, Two, Button My Shoe

Supplies: None

Skill: Running

Two parallel lines are drawn about 50 ft apart. One child is the leader and stands to one side. The rest of the children are behind one of the lines. The leader says "Ready." The following dialogue takes place between the leader and the children.
Children: One, two.

Leader: Button my shoe.

Children: Three, four.

Leader: Close the door.

Children: Five, six.

Leader: Pick up sticks.

Children: Seven, eight.

Leader: Run, or you'll be late!

As children carry on the conversation with the leader, they toe the line, ready to run. When the leader says the word late, children run to the other line and return. The first child across the original line is the winner and becomes the new leader. The leader can give the last response ("Run, or you'll be late!") in any timing she wishes--pausing or dragging out the words. No child is to leave before the word late is uttered.

Twins (Triplets)

Supplies: None

Skills: Body management

Formation: Scattered with partner

Youngsters find a space in the area. Each youngster has a partner (twin). The teacher gives commands such as "Take three hops and two leaps" or "Walk backward four steps and three skips." When the pairs are separated, the teacher says, "Find your twin!" Players find their twin and stand frozen back to back. The goal is to not be the last pair to find each other and assume the frozen position.

Students need to move away from each other during the movements. One alternative is to find a new twin each time. Another variation is to separate twins in opposite ends of the playing area.

Variation: The game becomes more challenging when played in groups of three (triplets). When using this variation, new partners should be selected each time.

Firefighter

Supplies: None

Skill: Running

A fire chief runs around the outside of a circle of children and taps a number of them on the back, saying "Firefighter" each time. After making the round of the circle, the chief goes to the center. When she says "Fire," the firefighters run counterclockwise around the circle and back to place. The one who returns first and is able to stand in place motionless is declared the winner and the new chief.

The chief can use other words to fool children, but they run only on the word Fire. This merely provides some fun, since there is no penalty for a false start. The circle children can sound the siren as the firefighters run.

Lesson Plans for Grades K-2 - Week 23
Fundamental Skills Using Balance Beams

Objectives:
To move to an even rhythm
To learn to balance the body while walking a beam
To manipulate an object while walking a beam

Equipment Required:
Six or 2"x4" boards (8 ft long)
Tom-tom
Hoops, wands, and beanbags for beam
activities

Instructional Activities	Teaching Hints

Introductory Activity -- European Running with Variations

Move to the rhythm throughout the area. Try some of the following challenges while moving.
1. Clap hands on various beats.
2. On signal, make a complete turn using four running steps.
3. On signal, scatter and run in general space. On next signal, resume circular running.
4. Stamp feet, say "hey!" and do a hop on stipulated beats.

Use the tom-tom or drum to teach moving to rhythm. Start the rhythm slowly and gradually increase the tempo.

Try moving in a scatter formation to a specified formation such as circle or line.

Fitness Development Activity --Fitness Games and Challenges

1. Stoop Tag.
2. Freeze; perform stretching activities.
3. Back-to-Back Tag.
4. Freeze; perform Abdominal Challenges using Curl-up variations.
5. Balance Tag.
6. Freeze; perform Arm-Shoulder Girdle Challenges using Push-up variations.
7. Elbow Swing Tag.
8. Freeze; perform Trunk Development challenges.
9. Color Tag.

Alternate simple tag games with fitness challenge activities. Exercise all parts of the body including upper body and abdominal strength and flexibility.

Any tag games can be used to stimulate movement. Play some student favorites.

Lesson Focus -- Fundamental Skills Using Balance Beams

Balance beam activities should be done using controlled walking movements. Speed of movement should always be avoided.

1. Practice walking on floor lines to establish qualities of controlled movement and not looking at feet.
2. Walk length of beam.
   a. Walk forward.
   b. Walk backward.
   c. Walk sideways--lead with both left and right sides of body.
   d. Try other steps--follow steps, heel and toe, on toes, etc.
3. Walk different directions and vary arm and body positions.
   a. Hands on hips.
   b. Hand on head.
   c. Arms folded across chest.
   d. Lean to one side or the other.
   e. Body bent forward or backward.
   f. Hands on knees or feet.
4. Perform animal movements across the balance beam.
   a. Puppy dog walk
   b. Bear Walk
   c. Crab Walk
5. Use manipulative equipment while walking the beam.
   a. Balance objects such as beanbags or wands while walking across beam.
   b. Step over a wand or through a hoop while walking the beam.
   c. Toss and catch a beanbag while walking the beam
   d. Twirl a hoop while walking the beam.
   e. Bounce a ball while walking a beam.
   f. Play catch with a partner while walking the beam.

If balance beams are not available, use 2" X 4" boards placed on the floor. This will give students some elevation off the floor and offer balance challenges.

Place the beams parallel to each other and have a similar number of students lined up behind each one. Students progress down the beam.

After moving the length of the beam, have students do a locomotor movement to the end of the teaching area and return. This will offer students both balance activities and the chance to practice locomotor movements. It also keeps students engaged in activity for a longer period of time and reduces standing and waiting time. Specified movements can be placed on return activity signs.

If a student steps off the beam, have them get back on and progress. Sometimes, students stop walking the beam and receive little practice.
Move with controlled, deliberate movements across the beam. Speed is not a goal.

Game Activity

Back to Back

Supplies: None

Skills: Fundamental locomotor movements

The number of children must be uneven. (If not, the teacher can play.) On signal, each child stands back to back with another child. One child will be without a partner. This child claps the hands for the next signal, and all children change partners, with the extra player from the previous game seeking a partner.

Variation: Considerably more activity can be achieved by putting in an extra command. After children are in partner formation back to back, the teacher says, "Everybody run [skip, hop, jump, slide]!" Other commands, such as "Walk like an elephant," can also be given. Children move around in the prescribed manner. When the signal is sounded, they immediately find a new partner and stand back to back.

Mousetrap

Supplies: None

Skills: Skipping, running, dodging

Half of the children form a circle with hands joined and face the center. This is the trap. The other children are on the outside of the circle. These are the mice. Three signals are given for the game. These can be word cues or other signals. On the first signal, the mice skip around, outside the circle, playing happily. On the second signal, the trap is opened. (The circle players raise their joined hands to form arches.) The mice run in and out of the trap. On the third signal, the trap snaps shut. (The arms come down.) All mice caught inside join the circle.

The game is repeated until all or most of the mice are caught. The players then exchange places, and the game begins anew. A child should not run in and out of the trap through adjacent openings.

Variation: This game is excellent with a parachute. The chute drops down and traps the mice.

Aviator

Supplies: None

Skills: Running, locomotor movements, stopping

Players are parked (in push-up position) at one end of the playing area. The air traffic controller (ATC) is in front of the players and calls out, "Aviators aviators, take off!" Youngsters take off and move like airplanes to the opposite side of the area. The first person to move to the other side and land the plane (get into push-up position facing the ATC) is declared the new ATC.

If the ATC yells out some type of stormy weather, all planes must return to the starting line and resume the parked position. Examples of stormy weather commands are lightning, thunder, hurricane, and tornado. Each ATC is allowed to give stormy weather warnings once.

Lesson Plans for Grades K-2 - Week 24
Manipulative Skills Using Hoops

Objectives:
To learn to move in an evasive fashion
To manipulate the hoop in a variety of challenges
To strike a ball with a bat

Equipment Required:
One hoop per child
Plastic bottle bat and ball
Batting tee (optional)

Instructional Activities	Teaching Hints

Introductory Activity – Marking

To teach marking, start by teaching partner tag. One partner moves whiles while the other partner attempts to tag him. Once tagged, the partners change roles and the other attempts to tag. Progress to marking which requires one of the partners to move in a desired fashion while the other attempts to stay near him. On signal, both partners freeze and cannot move their feet. The following partner tries to reach and touch (mark) the partner. If a mark is made, that partner receives a point. Resume the chase with the roles reversed.

The goal is not to play a chase game, but rather to dodge and change directions in order to evade their partner.

Remind students to run under control.

Fitness Development Activity --Walk, Trot, and Jog

Move to the following signals:
1. One drumbeat - walk.
2. Two drumbeats - trot.
3. Three drumbeats - jog.
4. Whistle - freeze and perform exercises.

Perform various strength and flexibility exercises between bouts of walk, trot, and jog. Examples are:
1. Bend and Twist
2. Sitting Stretch
3. Push-up challenges
4. Abdominal Challenges
5. Body Twist
6. Standing Hip Bend

Tape alternating segments (20 seconds in length) of silence and music to signal duration of exercise. Music segments indicate walk, trot, and jog activity. Intervals of silence signal performance of the strength and flexibility exercises.

See text, p. 174-186 for descriptions of exercises. Any exercises can be substituted. Try to maintain the balance of exercising all bodyparts.

Lesson Focus -- Manipulative Skills Using Hoops

1. Hula-hoop using various body parts such as waist, neck, knees, arms and fingers.
   a. While hula-hooping on the arms, try to change the hoop from one arm to the other.
   b. Change hoop from one partner to another while hula-hooping around the waist.
   c. Try leg skippers--hula-hoop with one leg and jump the hoop with the other leg.
   d. Hula-hoop around waist while on knees. While hooping, try to stand up and go back to knees.
   e. Exploratory activity.
2. Place the hoops on the floor to create various patterns. Have the children perform various fundamental locomotor movements and animal walks in, out of and between the hoops. Create different challenges by having students go in and out of various color hoops and specify a certain number of hoops they must enter.
3. Jump rope with the hoop--forward and backward. Begin with a back-and-forth pendulum swing. Try sideways jumping.
4. Thread the needle. Balance the hoop on head and try to step through the hoop. Do it forward, backward and sideways.
5. Roll hoop and run alongside it. Run ahead of it. Cross in front of it. Go through the hoop.
6. Spin the hoop like a top. How many times can you make it spin? How many times can you run around the spinning hoop before it falls?

Place the hoops around the perimeter of the area. Students move and pick up a hoop and begin practicing the assigned activity.

Encourage youngsters to find their personal space.

When learning to hula-hoop, teach youngsters to move the body part back and forth rather than in a circle. The natural tendency is to move the body part in a circle, making it impossible to keep the hoop circling.

Place the hoops on the floor when calling the class to attention. If students don't put the hoop on the floor, they will drop and disrupt the class.

7. Balance the hoop and then go through it before it falls.
8. For a change-of-pace activity, put hoops on floor. Perform various locomotor movements around many hoops. On signal, curl up inside a hoop. For challenge, have fewer hoops than students.
9. Roll hoop with a reverse spin to make it return to the thrower.
10. Reverse spin, catch on arm, and hula-hoop it. Try catching on foot.

The reverse spin can be taught by telling students to pull back and down toward the floor just prior to releasing the hoop.

Offer students a chance to perform their favorite activities.

Game Activity

Animal Tag

Supplies: None

Skills: Imagery, running, dodging

Two parallel lines are drawn about 40 ft apart. Children are divided into two groups, each of which takes a position on one of the lines. Children in one group get together with their leader and decide what animal they wish to imitate. Having selected the animal, they move over to within 5 ft or so of the other line. There they imitate the animal, and the other group tries to guess the animal correctly. If the guess is correct, they chase the first group back to its line, trying to tag as many as possible. Those caught must go over to the other team. The second group then selects an animal, and the roles are reversed. If the guessing team cannot guess the animal, however, the performing team gets another try. To avoid confusion, children must raise their hands to take turns at naming the animal. Otherwise, many false chases will occur. If children have trouble guessing, the leader of the performing team can give the initial of the animal.

Bottle Bat Ball

Supplies: A plastic bottle bat, whiffle ball, batting tee (optional), home plate, base marker

Skills: Batting, retrieving balls

Formation: Scattered

A home plate is needed, and a batting tee can be used. Foul lines should be marked wide enough so as not to be restrictive. The batter gets three pitches (or swings) to hit a fair ball, or she is out. The pitches are easy (as in slow-pitch softball), so that the batter has a good chance to hit the ball. The batter hits the ball and runs around the base marker and back to home. If the ball is returned to the pitcher's mound before the batter reaches home, she is out. (A marker should designate the pitcher's mound.) Otherwise, the batter has a home run and bats again. One fielder other than the pitcher is needed, but another can be used. The running distance to first base is critical. It can remain fixed or can be made progressively (one step) longer, until it reaches such a point that the fielders are heavily favored.

Teaching suggestion: The game should make use of a plastic bottle bat and fun (whiffle) ball. A rotation system should be established when an out is made.

Variation: A batting tee can be used.

Lesson Plans for Grades K-2 - Week 25
Movement Skills and Concepts (7)
Leaping, Jump Rope Targets, and Levels/Speed

Objectives:
To perform combinations of running and leaping steps
To move at different levels and speeds
To understand the concepts of acceleration and deceleration

Equipment Required:
One jump rope for each child
Tom-tom
Colored paper shapes for game

Instructional Activities	Teaching Hints

Introductory Activity --Locomotor Movement Variations

Using the basic locomotor movements and try the following variations:
1. Changes in speed
2. Weight bearing on different parts of foot (toes, heels, sides of feet)
3. Change directions
4. Making different patterns (triangles, squares, etc.)

The locomotor movements are walking, running, galloping, skipping, hopping jumping, leaping, and sliding.

Encourage students to put together sequences of various locomotor movements.

Fitness Development Activity --Animal Movements and Fitness Challenges

1. Puppy Dog Walk--30 seconds.
2. Freeze; perform stretching activities.
3. Measuring Worm Walk--30 seconds
4. Freeze; perform abdominal development challenges.
5. Seal Crawl–30 seconds.
7. Freeze; perform push-up position challenges.
8. Elephant Walk--30 seconds.
9. Injured Coyote Walk--30 seconds.
10. Freeze; perform abdominal challenges.
11. Crab Walk—30 seconds.
12. Rabbit Jump

See text, p. 167-168 for descriptions of animal walks.

Tape alternating segments (30 seconds in length) of silence and music to signal duration of exercise. Music segments indicate performing animal movements while intervals of silence announce doing the fitness challenges.

A variation is to place animal movement signs throughout the area and instruct students to move from sign to sign performing the appropriate animal movement each time they reach a new sign.

Lesson Focus -- Movement Skills and Concepts (7)

Fundamental Skill: Leaping (taking off on one foot and landing on the other)
1. Run in different directions and practice your leaping. Alternate the leading foot.
2. As you run, try a leap for good height; for distance; for both.
3. Explore the different arm positions you can use in leaping. Which is best? Try sailing through the air like an airplane.
4. Leap with a quarter or half turn.
5. If there are benches or other obstacles present, leap over these. Put several in succession for consecutive leaps.
6. Put one-half the children down scattered in curled position, face to the floor. The others leap over as many as possible.
7. Practice making two or three leaps in succession.
8. Practice Leap the Brook.

Select a few activities from each of the categories so students receive a variety of skills to practice. When possible, integrate the manipulative skill activities with fundamental skill activities. A common error is to teach all the activities from one category. The reason for multiple groups of activities is to provide variety and enhance motivation.

Use instructional cues to stimulate correct movement:
"Leap as far as possible."
"Lift with your arms."

Movement Concept: Levels and Speed
Find an area to move and explore the following:
1. Show me a slow, low level movement down and back.
2. What other ways can you go down and back at a slow, low level?
3. Change to a high level, fast movement.
4. What other ways can you do a high level, fast movement?
5. Combine a low, fast movement down with a high, slow movement back.
6. Explore other ways to move at different levels and speeds.

Explain the terms of speed and levels so children learn the concepts of altering movements.

Movement Concept: Partner Activity and Jump Rope Floor Targets

1. Jumping, hopping, cross-steps, scissors steps, heel clicks, etc.
2. Add quarter and half-turns, levels.
3. Take the weight partially on the hands; crouch jumps, bunny jump, cartwheel, etc.
4. Form a selected shape with the rope. Repeat 1, 2, 3. Form the same shape with your body.
5. Matching activity. One partner performs and the other matches the movement.
6. Partner activity. Join hands in some way; hop, jump, or use other movements down the rope or figure. Wheelbarrow or use partner-support activities and move down the rope.

Begin with the rope laid in a straight line along the floor and perform movements down the rope:

Emphasize not touching the rope while moving.

Movement Concept: Acceleration and Deceleration

Teach students what accelerate and decelerate mean.

1. Begin a movement and accelerate.
2. Begin with a fast movement and decelerate.
3. Accelerate to a fast speed and decelerate the same movement.
4. Accelerate with one movement to fast speed, shift to another movement, and decelerate.
5. Can you accelerate one movement of the body while decelerating another at the same time?

Suggested movements for practicing acceleration and deceleration: Stepping in place, running in place, circling body parts, arm thrust movements, jumping, hopping, changing stride, arm and leg movement while lying on back, pretending to be a locomotive engine of a railroad train.

Game Activity

Mix and Match

Supplies: None

Skills: Fundamental locomotor movements

A line is established through the middle of the area. Half of the children are on one side and half are on the other. There must be an odd person, the teacher or another child. The teacher gives a signal for children to move as directed on their side of the line. They can be told to run, hop, skip, or whatever. At another signal, children run to the dividing line, and each reaches across to join hands with a child from the opposite group. The goal is to not be left out. Children may reach over but may not cross the line. The person left out is moved to the opposite side so that players left out come from alternating sides of the area.

Variation: The game also can be done with music or a drumbeat, with the players rushing to the centerline to find partners when the rhythm stops.

Colors

Supplies: Colored paper (construction paper) cut in circles, squares, or triangles for markers (different color beanbags can be used also).

Skills: Color or other perceptual concepts, running

Five or six different-colored markers should be used, with a number of children having the same color. Children are standing or seated in a circle with a marker in front of each child. The teacher calls out a color, and everyone having that color runs counterclockwise around the circle and back to place. The first one seated upright and motionless is declared the winner. Different kinds of locomotor movement can be specified, such as skipping, galloping, walking, and so on. After a period of play, the children leave the markers on the floor and move one place to the left.

Variation: Shapes (e.g., circles, triangles, squares, rectangles, stars, and diamonds) can be used instead of colors, as can numbers or other articles or categories, such as animals, birds, or fish. This game has value in teaching identification and recognition.

Lesson Plans for Grades K-2 - Week 26
Tumbling, Stunts, and Animal Movements (3)

Objectives:
To understand safety considerations related to tumbling and inverted balances
To balance the body in a variety of situations
To perform individual self-testing stunts

Equipment Required:
Tumbling mats
Cones and signs for four-corners
    movement
Foam balls (8") for games

Instructional Activities	Teaching Hints

Introductory Activity -- Move, Perform Task on Signal

Do a locomotor movement; on signal, stop and perform a task. Suggested tasks are:
1. Seat Circles
2. Balances--foot, seat, and knee
3. Crab Kicks
4. Heel Clicks

Vary the locomotor movements by adding speed and level qualities.

Encourage students to perform their favorite task.

Fitness Development Activity --Four Corners Fitness

Outline a large rectangle with a cone at each corner. Place signs with movement tasks on both sides of the cones. Youngsters move around the outside of the rectangle and change movements as they pass each sign. The following movement activities are suggested for four signs:

Corner 1. Skipping/Jumping/Hopping
Corner 2. Sliding/Galloping
Corner 3. Various animal movements
Corner 4. Sport imitation movements

Stop the class after 30 seconds of movement and perform fitness challenges (See text, p. 163-167 for descriptions of challenges.)

Tape alternating segments of silence and music to signal duration of exercise. Music segments (30 seconds) indicate four corner aerobic activity while intervals of silence (45 seconds) announce performance of flexibility and strength development activities.

Faster moving students should pass on the outside of the rectangle.

The demands of the routine can be varied by increasing or decreasing the size of the rectangle.

Lesson Focus -- Tumbling, Stunts, and Animal Movements (3)

Animal Movement

Siamese Twin Walk

Stand back to back with a partner. Lock elbows. Walk forward, backward, and sideward in unison.

Tightrope Walk

Select a line, board, or chalked line on the floor as the high wire. Pretend to be on the high wire and do various tasks with exaggerated loss and control of balance. Add tasks such as jumping rope, juggling balls, and riding a bicycle. Pretend to hold a parasol or a balancing pole while performing.

Lame Dog Walk

Walk on both hands and one foot. Hold the other foot in the air as if injured. Walk a distance and change feet. The eyes should look forward. Move backward also and in other combinations. Try to move with an injured front leg.

Crab Walk

Squat down and reach back, putting both hands on the floor without sitting down. With head, neck, and body level, walk forward, backward, and sideward.

Five groups of activities in this lesson ensure that youngsters receive a variety of experiences. Pick a few activities from each group and teach them alternately. For example, teach one or two animal movements, then a tumbling and inverted balance, followed by a balance stunt, etc. Give equal time to each group of activities

Stunts and tumbling activities are self-testing activities in that each student has to overcome personal fear to accomplish many of the activities. This means that students should be encouraged to perform rather than forced.

Use many tumbling mats to avoid standing in line (3 or 4 students per mat).

Tumbling and Inverted Balances
Forward and Backward Roll review
   See previous lessons (#15 and #20)

Mountain Climber
   This activity is similar to the exercise known as the Treadmill. The weight is taken on the hands with one foot forward and one foot extended back, similar to a sprinter's start. When ready, the performer switches foot position with both feet moving simultaneously.

Switcheroo
   This Handstand lead-up activity begins in the front lunge position with the arms overhead. In one continuous movement, bend forward at the hips, place the hands on the mat, and invert the legs over the head. Do a scissors motion with the legs in the air, and then reverse the position of the feet on the mat. Repeat in a smooth and continuous motion.

Balance Stunts
Forward Balance
   Extend one leg backward until it is parallel to the floor. Keeping the eyes forward and the arms out to the sides, bend forward, balancing on the other leg. Hold for 5 seconds without moving. Reverse legs. (This is also called a Forward Scale.)

Hand-and-Knee Balance
   Get down on all fours, taking the weight on the hands, knees, and feet, with toes pointed backward. Lift one hand and the opposite knee. Keep the free foot and hand from touching during the hold. Reverse hand and knee positions.

Single-Knee Balance

   Perform the same action as in the previous stunt, but balance on one knee (and leg), with both arms outstretched to the sides. Use the other knee.

Individual Stunts
Turn-Over
   From a front-leaning rest position, turn over so that the back is to the floor. The body should not touch the floor. Continue the turn until the original position is reassumed. Reverse the direction. Turn back and forth several times.

Thread the Needle
   Touch the fingertips together in front of the body. Step through with one foot at a time while keeping the tips in contact. Step back to the original position. Next, lock the fingers in front of the body, and repeat the stunt. Finally, step through the clasped hands without touching the hands.

Heel Slap
   From an erect position with hands at the sides, jump upward and slap both heels with the hands.

Pogo Stick
   Pretend to be on a pogo stick by keeping a stiff body and jumping on the toes. Hold the hands in front as if grasping the stick. Progress in various directions.

Partner and Group Stunts
Double Top
   Face partner and join hands. Experiment to see which type of grip works best. With straight arms, lean away from each other and at the same time move the toes close to partner's. Spin around slowly in either direction, taking tiny steps.

Tumbling and inverted balances demand upper body strength. Therefore, students without adequate strength will not be able to safely complete the activities. Allow students to judge their ability.

This activity is a lead-up to the Handstand and teaches children to support the body weight briefly with the arms.

Overweight children are often at a disadvantage in this unit. Have empathy and patience for all students.

Balance activities are excellent activities to teach because all students are capable of performing them.

Encourage students to see how long they can hold the balances.

The body should be kept as rigid as possible throughout the turn.

Stress upward propelling action by the ankles and toes, with the body kept stiff, particularly at the knee joints.

Try a variation of the Double Top by doing it standing right side to right side.

Charlie Over the Water

Supplies: A volleyball or playground ball

Skills: Skipping, running, stopping, bowling (rolling)

The children are in circle formation with hands joined. One child, Charlie (or Sally, if a girl), is in the center of the circle, holding a ball. The children skip around the circle to the following chant.

Charlie over the water,

Charlie over the sea,

Charlie caught a bluebird,

But he can't catch me!

On the word <u>me</u>, Charlie tosses the ball in the air and children drop hands and scatter. When Charlie catches it, he shouts "Stop!" All of the children stop immediately and must not move their feet. Charlie rolls the ball in an attempt to hit one of the children. If he hits a child, that child becomes the new Charlie. If he misses, he must remain Charlie, and the game is repeated. If he misses twice, however, he picks another child for the center.

Circle Straddle Ball

Supplies: Two or more 8-in. foam balls

Skills: Ball rolling, catching

Children are in circle formation, facing in. Each stands in a wide straddle stance with the side of the foot against the neighbor's. The hands are on the knees. Two balls are used. The object of the game is to roll one of the balls between the legs of another player before he can get his hands down to stop the ball. Each time a ball goes between the legs of an individual, a point is scored. The players having the fewest points scored against them are the winners. Keep the circles small so students have more opportunities to handle the ball.

Teaching suggestion: The teacher should be sure that children catch and roll the ball, rather than batting it. Children must keep their hands on their knees until a ball is rolled at them. After some practice, the following variation can be played.

Variation: One child is in the center with a ball and is it. The other children are in the same formation as before. One ball is used. The center player tries to roll the ball through the legs of any child. She should mask her intent, using feints and changes of direction. Any child allowing the ball to go through his legs becomes it.

Flowers and Wind

Supplies: None

Skill: Running

Two parallel lines long enough to accommodate the children are drawn about 30 ft apart. Children are divided into two groups. One is the wind and the other the flowers. Each of the teams takes a position on one of the lines and faces the other team. The flowers secretly select the name of a common flower. When ready, they walk over to the other line and stand about 3 ft away from the wind. The players on the wind team begin to call out flower names--trying to guess the flower chosen. When the flower has been guessed, the flowers run to their goal line, chased by the players of the other team. Any player caught must join the other side. The roles are reversed and the game is repeated. If one side has trouble guessing, a clue can be given to the color or size of the flower or the first letter of its name.

Lesson Plans for Grades K-2 - Week 27
Rhythmic Movement (3)

Objectives:
To lead a group in marching activities
To independently travel the mini-challenge course
To move rhythmically and learn simple folk dances

Equipment Required:
Tom-tom
Tape player and music for rhythms
Equipment for mini-challenge course

Instructional Activities	Teaching Hints

Introductory Activity -- Drill Sergeant

Designate a student to be a drill sergeant. The sergeant then gives commands such as:
1. Walk, jog, and halt.
2. March, jump twice, and freeze (pose).
3. March, about face, and halt.
4. March, double time, and march in place.

The teacher can serve as the initial sergeant and then appoint a student to call the group to attention, give directions, and commands to move.

Teach the marching commands of about face, double time, etc.

Fitness Development Activity -- Mini-Challenge Course

Arrange four parallel courses with a group at each course. Students perform the challenges from a cone at the start to a finish cone and jog back to continuously repeat the course. On signal, groups rotate to a new course.

Course 1. Hop in and out of 5 hoops, Puppy Dog Walk around a cone for 5 seconds and skip to the finish cone.
Course 2. Weave in and out of four cones, Crab Walk around a cone for 5 seconds and gallop to finish cone.
Course 3. Do the Rolling Log the length of mat, do an agility run through 4 hoops, and slide to the finish cone.
Course 4. Jump over each of 5 cones, jump back and forth over a stretched out jump rope, run backwards around three cones; and hop to a cone.

Tape alternating segments (20 seconds in length) of silence and music to signal duration of exercise. Music segments indicate moving through the mini-challenge course while intervals of silence announce using the chute to enhance flexibility and strength development.

Students can set up their own mini-challenges.

Lesson Focus -- Rhythmic Movement (3)

Make dances easy for students to learn by implementing some of the following techniques:
1. Teach the dances without using partners.
2. Allow youngsters to move in any direction without left-right orientation.
3. Use scattered formation instead of circles.
4. Emphasize strong movements such as clapping and stamping to increase involvement.
5. Play the music at a slower speed when first learning the dance.

Rhythms should be taught like other sport skills. Avoid striving for perfection so students know it is acceptable to make mistakes. Teach a variety of dances rather than one or two in depth in case some students find it difficult to master a specific dance. Records can be ordered from Wagon Wheel Records, 17191 Corbina Lane #203, Huntington Beach, CA (714) 846-8169.

Shortnin' Bread (American)

Record: Kimbo 7050
Formation: Scattered with partner
Directions:

Measures	Action
1--2	Clap own hands
3--4	Pat partner's hands
5--6	Clap own hands
7--8	Slap own thighs
9--16	Repeat measures 1—8
17--20	Couples slide to the right holding hands.
21--24	Circle holding hands.
25--32	Repeat measures 17--24 moving to the left.

Children's Polka (German)

Records: HLP-4026; LS E-7; SD 1002

Formation: Single circle of couples, partners facing

Directions:

Measures Action

1--2   Two step-draw steps toward the center of the circle, ending with three steps in place. (Draw, draw, step, 2, 3)

3--4   Two step-draw steps away from the center, ending with three steps in place. (Draw, draw, step, 2, 3)

5--8   Repeat the pattern of measures 1--4.

9   Slap own knees once with both hands; clap own hands once. (Slap, clap)

10   Clap both hands with partner three times. (Clap, 2, 3)

11--12   Repeat the pattern of measures 9 and 10.

13   Hop, placing one heel forward, and shake the forefinger at partner three times. (Scold, 2, 3)

14   Repeat the "scolding" pattern with the other foot and hand. (Scold, 2, 3)

15--16   Turn once around in place with four running steps.

Jump Jim Jo (American)

Records: LS E-10; MAV 1041

Formation: Double circle, partners facing, both hands joined

Directions:

Measures Action

1--2   Do two jumps sideward, progressing counterclockwise, followed by three quick jumps in place. (Slow, slow, fast, fast, fast)

3--4   Release hands and turn once around in place with four jumps (two jumps per measure). Finish facing partner and rejoin hands. (Jump, turn, 3, 4)

5   Take two sliding steps sideward, progressing counterclockwise. (Slide, slide)

6   Partners face counterclockwise with inside hands joined and tap three times with the toe of the outside foot. (Tap, tap, tap)

7--8   Take four running steps forward, then face partner, join both hands, and end with three jumps in place. (Run, 2, 3, 4; Jump, 2, 3)

Jingle Bells, Var. 1 (Dutch)

Record: MAC 2046

Formation: Double circle, partners facing, with both hands joined

Directions: ·

Measures Action

1--2   Partners take eight slides counterclockwise. (Slide, 2, 3, . . . 8)

3--4   Partners turn so they are standing back to back, and take eight more slides in the line of direction. This move is best made by dropping the front hands and swinging the back hands forward until the dancers are standing back to back. They rejoin the hands that are now in back. Make this move with no loss of rhythm. (Slide, 2, 3, . . . 8)

5--6   Repeat the action of measures 1 and 2. To get back to the face-to-face position, let go of the back hands and swing the front hands backward, allowing the bodies to pivot and face again. (Slide, 2, 3, . . . 8)

7--8   Repeat measures 3 and 4. (Slide, 2, 3, . . . 8)

Chorus   Action

1   Clap own hands three times. (Clap own, 2, 3)

2   Clap both hands with partner three times. (Clap both, 2, 3)

3   Clap own hands four times. (Clap own, 2, 3, 4)

4   Clap both hands with partner once. (Clap both)

5--8   Right elbow swing with partner. Partners hook right elbows and swing clockwise with eight skips. (Swing, 2, 3, 4, 5, 6, 7, 8)

9--12   Repeat the clapping sequence of measures 1--4.

13--16 Left elbow swing with partner for eight skips, finishing in the original starting position, ready to repeat the entire dance with the same partner; or do a left elbow swing with partner for four skips, which is once around, then all children in the inner circle skip forward to the outer dancer ahead and repeat the entire dance from the beginning with a new partner. (Swing, 2, 3, 4, 5, 6, 7, 8)

Skunk Tag

Supplies: None

Skills: Fundamental locomotor movements, dodging

Children are scattered about the area. One child is it and chases the others, trying to tag one of them. When a tag is made, she says, "You're it." The new it chases other children. Children are safe when they move into the skunk position which is assumed by kneeling and reaching one arm under a knee and holding their nose. The skunk position can only be held for five seconds; students are then eligible to be tagged.

Aviator

Supplies: None

Skills: Running, locomotor movements, stopping

Players are parked (in push-up position) at one end of the playing area. The air traffic controller (ATC) is in front of the players and calls out, "Aviators aviators, take off!" Youngsters take off and move like airplanes to the opposite side of the area. The first person to move to the other side and land the plane (get into push-up position facing the ATC) is declared the new ATC.

If the ATC yells out some type of stormy weather, all planes must return to the starting line and resume the parked position. Examples of stormy weather commands are lightning, thunder, hurricane, and tornado. Each ATC is allowed to give stormy weather warnings once.

Right Angle

Supplies: Music

Skills: Rhythmic movement, body management

A tom-tom can be used to provide the rhythm for this activity. Some of the basic rhythm records also have suitable music. Children change direction at right angles on each heavy beat or change of music. The object of the game is to make the right-angle change on signal and not to bump into other players.

Lesson Plans for Grades K-2 - Week 28
Fundamental Skills Using Balance Beams with Equipment

Objectives:
To perform a variety of locomotor movements by choice
To perform balance skills while manipulating an object

Equipment Required:
Six or 2"x 4" boards (8 ft long)
Ball for game

Instructional Activities	Teaching Hints

Introductory Activity -- Secret Movement

Many different movements and/or combinations of movements are written on large flash cards. Without looking, the teacher or a student selects a card and directs the class to "show me" the secret movement. Youngsters select a movement and perform it until signaled to stop. The card is then revealed to the class to see which youngsters, by chance, guessed the secret movement.

Use the basic locomotor movements when first teaching Secret Movements.

Use a variety of movements such as animal walks, stunts, exercises, and sport imitation activities for variety.

Fitness Development Activity --Fitness Games and Challenges

1. Stoop Tag.
2. Freeze; perform stretching activities.
3. Back-to-Back Tag.
4. Freeze; perform Abdominal Challenges using Curl-up variations.
5. Balance Tag.
6. Freeze; perform Arm-Shoulder Girdle Challenges using Push-up variations.
7. Elbow Swing Tag.
8. Freeze; perform Trunk Development challenges.
9. Color Tag.

Alternate simple tag games (See text, p. 168-169) with fitness challenge activities. Exercise all parts of the body including upper body and abdominal strength and flexibility.

Assign many students to be it. Allow a student to quit being "it" if they so choose.

Lesson Focus - Balance Beam Activities with Manipulative Equipment

Using Beanbags
1. Try some of the following steps forward, backward and sideways:
   a. Walk
   b. Follow steps
   c. Heel and Toe
   d. Side or Draw Step
   e. Tip Toes
   f. Grapevine
2. Try with beanbag on head and different arm positions:
   a. On hips
   b. On knees
   c. Arms behind Back
   d. Arms folded across chest
   e. Arms pointing toward ceiling
3. Move across the beam using animal walks.

Using Hoops
1. Carry a hoop on various body parts while moving across the beam.
2. Step through a self-held hoop while walking beam.
3. Step through a hoop held by a partner.
4. Hula-hoop around waist while moving across the beam.
5. Twirl a hoop around different body parts and proceed across the beam.

Using Playground Balls
1. Walk across the beam and dribble the ball on the floor.
2. Walk across the beam and toss and catch the ball.
3. Walk across the beam and toss the ball back and forth overhead.
4. Walk across the beam with the ball held between the knees.

If balance beams are not available, use 2" X 4" boards placed on the floor. This will give students some elevation off the floor and offer balance challenges.

Place the beams parallel to each other and have a similar number of students lined up behind each one. Students progress down the beam.

After moving the length of the beam, have students do a locomotor movement to the end of the teaching area and return. This will offer students both balance activities and the chance to practice locomotor movements. It also keeps students engaged in activity for a longer period of time and reduces standing and waiting time. Specified movements can be placed on return activity signs.

If the challenges are too difficult, allow students the opportunity to move across the beam without having to manipulate equipment. Allow students to choose challenges they feel capable of performing.

Squirrel in the Trees

Supplies: None

Skills: Fundamental locomotor movements

A number of trees are formed by two players facing each other and holding hands or putting hands on each other's shoulders. A squirrel is in the center of each tree, and one or two extra squirrels are outside. A signal to change is given. All squirrels move out of their tree to another tree, and the extra players try to find a free tree. Only one squirrel is allowed in a tree. Teaching suggestion: As a system of rotation, when each squirrel moves into a tree, he can change places with one of the players forming the tree. The rotation is important, because it ensures that all children eventually are active.

Stop Ball

Supplies: A ball

Skills: Tossing, catching

One child, with hands over the eyes, stands in the center of a circle of children. A ball is tossed clockwise or counterclockwise from child to child around the circle. Failing to catch the ball or making a bad toss incurs a penalty. That child must take one long step back and stay out of the game for one turn.

At a time of her own selection, the center player calls, "Stop." The player caught with the ball steps back and stays out for one turn. The center player should be allowed three or four turns and then be changed.

Lesson Plans for Grades K-2 - Week 29
Movement Skills and Concepts (8)
Pushing, Pulling, Rope Jumping, and Balancing the Body

Objectives:
To make a variety of shapes with the body
To know the difference between pushing and pulling
To know the mechanics of effective pushing and pulling
To understand the difference between making circles with body parts and twisting

Equipment Required:
One jump rope for each student
Tom-tom
Plastic bottle bat and ball
Batting tee

Instructional Activities	Teaching Hints

Introductory Activity -- Run and Assume Shape

Place emphasis on making a variety of shapes and balances. Vary the locomotor movements.
1. Run and move to a prone (one drumbeat) or supine (two drumbeats) position on signal.
2. Run and move into a balance position.
3. Run and freeze in various shapes.

Place emphasis on running under control and assuming specified shape quickly.

Have students move into the activity area in scatter formation.

Fitness Development Activity --Walk, Trot, and Jog

Move to the following signals:
   1.One drumbeat - walk.
   2.Two drumbeats - trot.
   3.Three drumbeats - jog.
   4.Whistle - freeze and perform exercises.

Use various strength and flexibility exercises between bouts of walk, trot, and jog to allow students to recover aerobically. Examples are:
   1. Bend and Twist
   2. Sitting Stretch
   3. Push-up challenges
   4. Abdominal Challenges
   5. Body Twist
   6. Standing Hip Bend

Tape alternating segments (20 seconds in length) of silence and music to signal duration of exercise. Music segments indicate walk, trot, and jog activity. Intervals of silence signal performance of the strength and flexibility exercises.

Encourage students to move around the area in the same direction.

See text, p. 174-186 for descriptions of exercises. Any exercises can be substituted. Try to exercise all bodyparts.

Lesson Focus - Movement Skills and Concepts (8)

Fundamental Skill: Pushing
1. Push against a wall first in an erect position and then with knees bent and one foot braced behind the other. Which is better
2. Push an imaginary object that is very light. Now try pushing a very heavy object.
3. Try to push a partner who is sitting on the floor
4. Can you push an object with your feet without using your arms and hands? Try with the hands braced behind you.
5. Put your back against an object and push with your feet.
6. Explore different ways to push your object.
7. Find a friend to explore different ways to push him or her over a line.
8. Sit down back to back with your partner and see whether you can move him or her.
9. Lie on the floor and push yourself backward, forward, sideways. Which is easiest?
10. Lie on the floor and push yourself forward with one hand and one foot. Which hand-foot combination is best?
11. Show how you can push a ball to a friend. Push slowly and steadily.

Select a few activities from each of the categories so students receive a variety of skills to practice. When possible, integrate the manipulative skill activities with fundamental skill activities. A common error is to teach all the activities from one category. The reason for multiple groups of activities is to provide variety and enhance motivation.

Use instructional cues such as:
   "Use a wide stance"
   "Bend your knees and lower your center of gravity"
   "Place all of your body behind your hands while pushing"

Fundamental Skill: Pulling

1. Reach for an imaginary object near the ceiling and pull the object toward you quickly. Now slowly and smoothly.
2. Clasp your hands together and pull against each hand as hard as you can. Vary the positions of the arms.
3. Hold hands with your partner and try to pull against each other balancing on one foot.
4. Hold hands with partner, drop low, and pull hard against each other.
5. Have partner sit down. Pull partner slowly by the feet.
6. Pretend to pull a heavy object while you are lying on the floor.
7. With partner seated on the floor, pull him or her to his or her feet.

Use instructional cues to enhance pulling skills:
> "Lower your body and widen your base of support"
> "Lean away from the source of pull"

Use slow controlled pulling. Remind youngsters to ask their partner to stop if the hand grip is slipping.

Manipulative Skills: Rope Jumping

Encourage children to work on needed skill areas. Suggest working first without music and then with music.

Allow students time to practice new jumping skills. Find students who can demonstrate different skills if necessary.

Movement Concepts: Circles in the Body

1. How many joints of the body can do circular motion (circles)?
2. How many different ways can you make the arms circle, using both arms at once?
3. Lie on your back, lift your legs. Can you make the arms and legs go in circles? Can you make them go in different circles?
4. In a standing position, show arm circles in horizontal, vertical and diagonal direction using one arm at a time.
5. Repeat item 4, using both arms.
6. Lie on back and lift the legs. Make circles with the feet first singly and then together.
7. Explore different ways to make two different body parts make circles in different directions.
8. Make a large circle with one part of the body and a small one with another.
9. What joints can twist as well as circle?

Explain that a joint is where different body parts are connected.

Explain the terms horizontal, vertical, and diagonal.

Encourage students to make different size circles in many different directions.

Explain the difference between twisting and circling.

Movement Concept: Balancing the Body

1. On different parts of the body.
2. On different number of body parts, varying from one through five. Different combinations.
3. Balancing on different levels.
4. Work out a sequence of three or four balance poses. Flow from one to the next.
5. Try to balance on both hands.
6. With a partner, form different balances.

Balance skills should emphasize smooth movements that are held 3 to 5 seconds. Students will always try to speed up the balance activity if they are having trouble maintaining balance.

Share balance innovations with peers.

Movement Concept: Sports Imitation Activities

1. Pretend you are a football player --kicking the ball, passing the ball, making a tackle, centering the ball.
2. Pretend you are a basketball player--shooting a basket, dribbling, guarding, jump ball, a free throw shot.
3. Let's pretend you are a track and field star performing at: the shot-put, the javelin throw, or the discus. Move like a hurdler.
4. Pretend you are a baseball player--pitching, catching a fly ball, fielding a grounder and throwing to first, batting, bunting, sliding into a base.

If desired, pictures of athletes can be used to motivate movement.

Place emphasis on performing the activities with speed and authenticity. Some students may need to see demonstrations of how the skills should be performed.

Game Activity

Change Sides

Supplies: None
Skill: Body management

Two parallel lines are established 30 ft apart. Half of the children are on each line. On signal, all cross to the other line, face the center, and stand at attention. The first group to do this correctly wins a point. Children must be cautioned to use care when passing through the opposite group. They should be spaced well along each line; this allows room for them to move through each group. The locomotor movements should be varied. The teacher may say, "Ready--walk!" Skipping, hopping, long steps, sliding, and other forms of locomotion can be specified. The position to be assumed at the finish can be varied also.

Bottle Bat Ball

Supplies: A plastic bottle bat, whiffle ball, batting tee (optional), home plate, base marker

Skills: Batting, retrieving balls

A home plate is needed, and a batting tee can be used. Foul lines should be marked wide enough so as not to be restrictive.

The batter gets three pitches (or swings) to hit a fair ball, or she is out. The pitches are easy (as in slow-pitch softball), so that the batter has a good chance to hit the ball. The batter hits the ball and runs around the base marker and back to home. If the ball is returned to the pitcher's mound before the batter reaches home, she is out. (A marker should designate the pitcher's mound.) Otherwise, the batter has a home run and bats again. One fielder other than the pitcher is needed, but another can be used. The running distance to first base is critical. It can remain fixed or can be made progressively (one step) longer, until it reaches such a point that the fielders are heavily favored.

Teaching suggestion: The game should make use of a plastic bottle bat and fun (whiffle) ball. A rotation system should be established when an out is made.

Variation: A batting tee can be used.

Lesson Plans for Grades K-2 - Week 30
Walking and Jogging Skills

Objectives:
To walk and/or jog at a continuous and personalized pace
To understand the benefits of aerobic activity

Equipment Required:
Parachute
Equipment for games

Instructional Activities	Teaching Hints
Introductory Activity -- Simple Games	

Use a game that requires little teaching and much gross motor activity. The following are suggested:
  1. Back to Back, (see Lesson plan, p. 2)
  2. Twins, (see Lesson plan, p. 54)
  3. Change Sides, (see Lesson plan, p. 9)
	Back to Back and Twins are excellent for teaching youngsters to find a partner quickly. Change Sides teaches youngsters to move across the teaching area without bumping into others.

Fitness Development Activity -- Parachute Fitness	
1. Jog while holding the chute in the left hand. (music) 2. Shake the chute. (no music) 3. Slide while holding the chute with both hands. (music) 4. Sit and perform curl-ups. (no music) 5. Skip. (music) 6. Freeze, face the center, and stretch the chute tightly. Repeat five to six times. (no music) 7. Run in place while holding the chute taut at different levels. (music) 8. Sit with legs under the chute. Do a seat walk toward the center. Return to the perimeter. Repeat four to six times. (no music) 9. Place the chute on the ground. Jog away from the chute and return on signal. Repeat. (music) 10. Move into push-up position holding the chute with one hand. Shake the chute. (no music) 11. Shake the chute and jump in place. (music) 12. Lie on back with feet under the chute. Shake the chute with the feet. (no music) 13. Hop to the center of the chute and return. (music) 14. Sit with feet under the chute. Stretch by touching the toes with the chute. Relax with other stretches while sitting. (no music)	Tape alternating segments (20 seconds in length) of silence and music to signal duration of exercise. Music segments indicate aerobic activity with the parachute while intervals of silence announce using the chute to enhance flexibility and strength development. Space youngsters evenly around the chute. Use different hand grips (palms up, down, mixed). All movements should be done under control. Some of the faster and stronger students will have to moderate their performance.

Lesson Focus -- Walking and Jogging

The walking and jogging lesson offers emphasis on developing activity patterns that can be used outside of the school environment. An educational approach to this lesson teaches students that walking and jogging is a personal activity that offers excellent health benefits. It is an activity that can literally be done for a lifetime. The following are suggestions for implementing this unit of instruction:

1. Youngsters should be allowed to find a friend with whom they want to jog or walk. The result is usually a friend of similar ability level. A way to judge correct pace is to be able to talk with a friend without undue stress. If students are too winded to talk, they are probably running too fast. A selected friend will encourage talking and help assure that the experience is positive and within the student's aerobic capacity. *Pace, not race* is the motto.

2. Jogging and walking should be done in any direction so people are unable to keep track of the distance covered. Doing laps on a track can be discouraging for less able youngsters. They usually finish last and are open to chiding by the rest of the class.

3. Jogging and walking should be done for a specified time rather than a specified distance. All youngsters should not have to run the same distance. This goes against the philosophy of accompanying individual differences and varying aerobic capacities. Running or walking for a set amount of time will allow less able students to do the best they can without fear of ridicule.

4. Teachers should not be concerned about foot action, since the child selects naturally the means that is most comfortable. Arm movement should be easy and natural, with elbows bent. The head and upper body should be held up and back. The eyes look ahead. The general body position in walking and jogging should be erect but relaxed. Jogging on the toes should be avoided.

5. Jogging and walking should not be a competitive, timed activity. Each youngster should move at a self-determined pace. Racing belongs in the track program. Another reason to avoid speed is that racing keeps youngsters from learning to pace themselves. For developing endurance and gaining health benefits, it is more important to move for a longer time at a slower speed than to run at top speed for a shorter distance.

6. It can be motivating for youngsters if they run with a piece of equipment, i.e., beanbag or jump rope. They can play catch with a beanbag or roll a hoop while walking or jogging.

Game Activity

Low Organization Games

When the jogging activity is finished, students may be somewhat fatigued. Play games that do not place high demand on the cardiovascular system.

Lesson Plans for Grades K-2 - Week 31
Throwing Skills (2)

Objectives:
To demonstrate a variety of balance positions
To throw a ball using the overhand technique
To throw with velocity using side orientation and opposition

Equipment Required:
Yarnballs
Rag balls or tennis balls
Hoops, boxes or mats for targets
Music and tape for circuit training

Instructional Activities	Teaching Hints
Introductory Activity -- Move, Freeze, and Balance	
Students move throughout the instructional area using a specified locomotor movement. On signal they freeze in a unique balance position.	Encourage a wide variety of balance positions. Balance positions using the hands should also be reinforced.
Fitness Development Activity --Circuit Training	
Make signs, put them on cones and place around the perimeter of the teaching area. Students perform the exercise specified at each station while the music is playing.	Tape alternating segments of silence and music to signal duration of exercise.
1. Tortoise and Hare	Music segments (begin at 30 seconds)
2. Curl-up challenges	indicate activity at each station while
3. Hula Hooping on arms	intervals of silence (10 seconds)
4. Standing Hip Bend	announce it is time to stop and move
5. Agility run--run back and forth between two designated lines	forward to the next station.
6. Push-up challenges	
7. Crab Walk	See text, p. 174-186 for descriptions of
8. Bend and Twist	exercises.

Lesson Focus -- Throwing Skills (2)

Mimetics
1. Cue students and model a good throw.
   a. Use terms such as "wind-up," "turn your non-throwing side to the target," "step toward the target, follow through."
   b. *Encourage* children to throw *hard*.
   c. Use skilled student throwers to model good throws.

Emphasize lifting the throwing arm and pointing at the target with the non-throwing arm.

Make a "T" with your arms in preparation to throw (both arms extended to sides at shoulder level).

Station Format
1. Activities emphasizing form.
   a. Standing on a tumbling mat
      Throwers stand on the edge of the mat and step off the mat (with the foot opposite the throwing arm) as they throw toward the wall. (The other foot remains on the mat.)
   b. Both feet in hoop.
      Throwers begin in a side-facing position to the target, with both feet inside the hoop; they then step outside of the hoop with the foot opposite the throwing arm and throw to the wall.
   c. Cone behind the student.
      The student must touch the cone with the throwing hand on the back-swing, then throw to the wall.

Focus on throwing form and the velocity of the throw rather than accuracy.

Emphasize throwing hard! Proper form can only be learned when students are encouraged to throw as hard as possible.

Cue students to move their throwing hand behind their head before the throw.

Using large targets (focus on velocity, not accuracy):
1. Throw at a wall or fence.
   a. Throw tennis or rag balls hard from 15-20 ft.
   b. Retrieve the balls after all have been thrown.
2. Throw at cardboard boxes near a fence (the noise from a good hit is reinforcing).
3. Throw at hoops leaning against a wall or fence.
4. Throw at bowling pins which make noise when they fall (audio reinforcement).
5. Throw for distance. Encourage students to throw as far as possible. Reinforce distance and throwing hard.

Give each student 4 or 5 balls to throw. They can be placed in a frisbee to keep them from rolling around. When all the balls have been thrown by all the students, students go retrieve the same number of balls they have thrown.

When students throw for accuracy, they usually regress to an immature form of throwing. Reinforce distance, velocity, and throwing hard.

Game Activity

Animal Tag

Supplies: None

Skills: Imagery, running, dodging

Two parallel lines are drawn about 40 ft apart. Children are divided into two groups, each of which takes a position on one of the lines. Children in one group get together with their leader and decide what animal they wish to imitate. Having selected the animal, they move over to within 5 ft or so of the other line. There they imitate the animal, and the other group tries to guess the animal correctly. If the guess is correct, they chase the first group back to its line, trying to tag as many as possible. Those caught must go over to the other team. The second group then selects an animal, and the roles are reversed. If the guessing team cannot guess the animal, however, the performing team gets another try. To avoid confusion, children must raise their hands to take turns at naming the animal. Otherwise, many false chases will occur. If children have trouble guessing, the leader of the performing team can give the initial of the animal.

Forest Ranger

Supplies: None

Skill: Running

Half of the children form a circle and face the center. These are the trees. The other half of the children are forest rangers and stand behind the trees. An extra child, the forest lookout, is in the center. The forest lookout starts the game by calling, "Fire in the forest. Run, run, run!" Immediately, the forest rangers run around the outside of the circle to the right. After a few moments, the lookout steps in front of one of the trees. This is the signal for each of the rangers to step in front of a tree. One player is left out, and she becomes the new forest lookout. The trees become rangers and the rangers become trees. Each time the game is played, the circle must be moved out somewhat, because the formation narrows when the rangers step in front of the trees.

Lesson Plans for Grades K-2 - Week 32
Fundamental Skills Using Parachute Activity

Objectives:
To perform strength development activities with the parachute
To cooperate with peers in parachute activities

Equipment Required:
Parachute
Tom-tom
Colored paper in shapes for game
10-20 beanbags for game

Instructional Activities	Teaching Hints

Introductory Activity -- European Running with Equipment

Review European running (moving to the beat of a tom-tom) and emphasize the following points:
1. Move to the rhythm
2. Lift the knees and trot
3. Maintain proper spacing between each other

After the review, give each child a beanbag or playground ball. Every fourth step, toss the beanbag upward or bounce the ball.

European running should be started with a walking step to the beat of the tom-tom. Gradually speed up the tempo of the rhythm as students become competent.

Fitness Development Activity -- Walk, Trot, and Jog

Move to the following signals:
1. One drumbeat - walk.
2. Two drumbeats - trot.
3. Three drumbeats - jog.
4. Whistle - freeze and perform exercises.

Perform various strength and flexibility exercises between bouts of walk, trot, and jog. Examples are:
1. Bend and Twist
2. Sitting Stretch
3. Push-up Challenges
4. Abdominal Challenges
5. Body Twist
6. Standing Hip Bend

Tape alternating segments (20 seconds in length) of silence and music to signal duration of exercise. Music segments indicate walk, trot, and jog activity. Intervals of silence signal performance of the strength and flexibility exercises.

See text, p. 174-186 for descriptions of exercises. Any exercises can be substituted. Try to maintain the balance of exercising all bodyparts.

Lesson Focus -- Fundamental Skills Using Parachute Activity

1. Circular movements.
   Move utilizing locomotor movements and holding the chute at various levels--walk, run, hop, jump, skip, slide, draw steps.
2. Shaking the Rug and Making Waves.
   Shaking the Rug should involve small, rapid movements, whereas Making Waves is large movements.
3. Making a Dome.
   Parachute should be on the floor and held with both hands. Make a dome by standing up and rapidly lifting the chute overhead.
4. Mushroom.
   Similar to the Dome except three or four steps toward the center are taken by each student.
   a. Mushroom Release--all students release the chute at its peak of inflation.
   b. Mushroom Run--Make a mushroom, students move toward center; a few selected students release grip, and run around the inside of the chute back to place.
5. Activities with Balls and Beanbags.
   a. Ball Circle--Use a basketball or cageball and make it circle around the outside of the chute. Add a second ball.
   b. Popcorn--Place six to ten whittle balls on the chute and shake them into the air.
   c. Giant Popcorn--Use beachballs instead of whiffle balls.

When performing locomotor movements with the chute, have students hold the chute with one hand. The direction of the movement can be stated by asking for a "right hand run," or a "left hand skip" etc.

When making a dome, have all students on one knee with both hands on the floor. On signal they make a strong movement upward.

Encourage all students to work together. Discuss how much easier it is when all students pull and lift together.

Try the activities holding the chute with both hands and with one hand.

d. Poison Snake--Place six to ten jump ropes on the chute. Divide the players in half. Try to shake the ropes so they touch a player on the opposing team.

Play the poison snake activity like a tag game. If the jump rope touches a player, they must release their grip and back away from the chute. Reset the game and start over with all players playing.

6. Kite Run.

Half the class holds the chute on one side. They run in any direction together and as fast as possible. The parachute should trail like a kite.

7. Tug-of-War.

Divide the class into two equal halves. On signal, they pull and try to move each other.

8. Hole in One.

Use six or eight small balls of two different colors. The objects is to get the other team's balls to fall through the hole in the center.

Playing hole in one is a challenge. Use many balls so the odds of a ball going into the center are increased.

9. Ocean Walk.

The class is on their knees, making waves with the chute. Three or four youngsters are selected to walk or jog "in the ocean" without falling.

Safety is important when walking on the parachute. The chute must not be lifted.

Game Activity

May I Chase You?

Supplies: None

Skills: Running, dodging

The class stands behind a line long enough to accommodate all. The runner stands about 5 ft in front of the line. One child in the line asks, "May I chase you?" The runner replies, "Yes, if you are wearing ," naming a color, an article of clothing, or a combination of the two. All who qualify immediately chase the runner until she is tagged. The tagger becomes the new runner. Children can think of other ways to identify those who may run.

Tommy Tucker's Land

Supplies: About ten beanbags for each game

Skills: Dodging, running

One child, Tommy or Tammi Tucker, stands in the center of a 15-ft square, within which the beanbags are scattered. Tommy is guarding his land and the treasure. The other children chant, "I'm on Tommy Tucker's land, picking up gold and silver." Children attempt to pick up as much of the treasure as they can while avoiding being tagged by Tommy. Any child who is tagged must return the treasure and retire from the game. The game is over when only one child is left or when all of the beanbags have been successfully filched. The teacher may wish to call a halt to the game earlier if a stalemate is reached. In this case, the child with the most treasure becomes the new Tommy.

Variation: This game can be played with a restraining line instead of a square, but there must be boundaries that limit movement.

Colors

Supplies: Colored paper (construction paper) cut in circles, squares, or triangles for markers

Skills: Color or other perceptual concepts, running

Five or six different-colored markers should be used, with a number of children having the same color. Children are standing or seated in a circle with a marker in front of each child. The teacher calls out a color, and everyone having that color runs counterclockwise around the circle and back to place. The first one seated upright and motionless is declared the winner. Different kinds of locomotor movement can be specified, such as skipping, galloping, walking, and so on. After a period of play, the children leave the markers on the floor and move one place to the left.

Variation: Shapes (e.g., circles, triangles, squares, rectangles, stars, and diamonds) can be used instead of colors, as can numbers or other articles or categories, such as animals, birds, or fish. This game has value in teaching identification and recognition.

Lesson Plans for Grades K-2 - Week 33
Movement Skills and Concepts (9)
Bending, Stretching, and Weight Transfer

Objectives:
To understand the difference between bending and stretching
To bend and stretch in many different ways
To be able to transfer weight from one body part to another

Equipment Required:
Four corners signs and cones
Parachute

Instructional Activities	Teaching Hints

Introductory Activity -- Bridges and Walls

Students work in pairs with one partner making a bridge and the other waiting to move. On signal, the standing partner runs to a wall, back to and under his/her partner's bridge. The pattern (to a wall and back under) continues until the teacher signals a switch.

Place emphasis on not touching the bridge when moving under.

Encourage the use of different locomotor movements.

Fitness Development Activity -- Four Corners Fitness

Outline a large rectangle with a cone at each corner. Place signs with movement tasks on both sides of the cones. Youngsters move around the outside of the rectangle and change movements as they pass each sign. The following movement activities are suggested:

Corner 1. Skipping/Jumping/Hopping
Corner 2. Sliding/Galloping
Corner 3. Various animal movements
Corner 4. Sport imitation movements

Stop the class after 30 seconds of movement and perform fitness challenges See text, p. 163-167 for descriptions of challenges.

Tape alternating segments of silence and music to signal duration of exercise. Music segments (30 seconds) indicate four corner aerobic activity while intervals of silence (45 seconds) announce performance of flexibility and strength development activities.

Faster moving students should pass on the outside of the rectangle.

The demands of the routine can be varied by increasing or decreasing the size of the rectangle.

Lesson Focus -- Movement Skills and Concepts (9)

Fundamental Skill: Bending
1. Can you bend forward and up?
2. Show how far you can bend backward. Can you see behind you on your backward bend?
3. Combine a forward bend with a backward bend.
4. Bend right and left. Try with your hands out to the sides. Overhead.
5. Explore different ways the body can bend in a standing position.
6. Sit down. How does this affect the bending possibilities of the body? Can you bend forward so your chin touches the floor?
7. How many body parts (joints) can you bend below the waist? Above the waist?
8. Who can lie down and bend two, three, four, five, six parts?
9. Pick two similar parts. Bend one while unbending the other.
10. Pick two body parts (joints). Beginning at the same time, bend one quickly and one slowly. Bend one smoothly and one with jerks.
11. Make a familiar shape by bending two body parts.
12. Show how you can bend to look funny, happy, sad, slow, and quick.

Select a few activities from each of the categories so students receive a variety of skills to practice. When possible, integrate the manipulative skill activities with fundamental skill activities. A common error is to teach all the activities from one category. The reason for multiple groups of activities is to provide variety and enhance motivation.

Teach the various joints that are bent with different movements.

Explain the difference between bending and stretching.

Fundamental Skill: Stretching
1. Stretch as many body parts as you can.
2. Stretch your arms, legs and feet in as many ways as possible.
3. At the same time stretch your feet in one direction and your arms in another.
4. Stretch one body part quickly, slowly, smoothly. Try another. Repeat.
5. Bend a body part and tell me which muscles or muscle groups are being stretched.

Encourage smooth controlled stretching. Use cues such as smoothly, gently, without jerking, etc.

6. How many ways can you stretch while sitting on the floor?
7. Lie on the floor (prone or supine) and stretch two parts at once. Add others up to five.
8. From any position you like, see if you can at the same time stretch one part quickly (but smoothly) and one part slowly. Try one part quickly and two parts slowly.
9. From a kneeling position, set a mark on the floor where you can reach (stretch) without losing balance. Increase the distance.
10. Stretch your one arm while your other curls (bends). Reverse.
11. Can you stretch as tall as a giraffe? As wide as an elephant? As long as a snake?
12. Can you stretch the muscles in your chest, back, ankles, wrist, and fingers? Is this easy?

Help youngsters understand what muscles are being stretched. They can tell by feeling which muscles are tight and hard.

Discuss why people stretch - to maintain flexibility and be able to have a full range of motion in all joints.

Discuss how adults stretch their muscles prior to vigorous activity.

Manipulative Skill: Parachute Activities
Use locomotor activities with the parachute as the prior activities (bending and stretching) are non-moving activities. See the previous Lesson Plan #32, p. 76-77 for many parachute activities.

The parachute activity should place emphasis on locomotor movements since the other parts of the lesson are somewhat inactive.

Movement Concept: Receiving and Transferring Weight
1. Project yourself high into the air and land. Try to land now with as little noise as possible.
2. Practice projecting yourself into the air and landing in different fashions.
3. Experiment with different landings where one or both hands touch the floor at the completion of the landing.
4. Experiment with turns as you land.
5. Begin your movement through the air with a short run and practice landings.
6. Take a position with the body balanced on two different parts. Transfer the weight to another two parts. Go from three to three.
7. Transfer the weight from a rounded part of the body to the hands and/or the feet. Go back to the rounded part.
8. Jump and land under control. Transfer the weight to another two body parts.
9. Explore different combinations of transferring the weight from various parts to others.

Weight transfer is used in movement to create force. Use throwing as an example of transferring the weight from the rear foot to the forward foot.

Bend the knees when absorbing force from weight transfer. Bent joints are like springs and reduce the chance of injury to joints.

Game Activity

Marching Ponies
     Supplies: None
     Skills: Marching, running
     One child, the ringmaster, crouches in the center of a circle of ponies formed by the other children. Two goal lines on opposite sides of the circle are established as safe areas. The ponies march around the circle in step, counting as they do so. At a predetermined number (whispered to the ringmaster by the teacher), the ringmaster jumps up and attempts to tag the others before they can reach the safety lines. Anyone tagged joins the ringmaster in the center and helps catch the other children the next time. The game should be reorganized after six to eight children have been caught. Those left in the circle are declared the winners.
Variation: Other characterizations, such as lumbering elephants, jumping kangaroos, and the like, can be tried. A child who suggests a unique movement could be allowed to be the ringmaster.

Cat and Mice
     Supplies: None
     Skills: Running, dodging
   Children form a large circle. One child is the cat and four others are the mice. The cat and mice cannot leave the circle. On signal, the cat chases the mice inside the circle. As they are caught, the mice join the circle. The last mouse caught becomes the cat for the next round. Make sure each student gets a chance to be in the center. Sometimes, one child has difficulty catching the last mouse or any of the mice. If this is the case, children forming the circle can take a step toward the center, thus constricting the running area. The teacher should cut off any prolonged chase sequence.

Lesson Plans for Grades K-2 - Week 34
Rhythmic Movement (4)

Objectives:
To move rhythmically in simple folk dances
To accept the outcomes of game activities
To show consideration for others in a variety of situations

Equipment Required:
Parachute
Music for dances and tape recorder
Yardstick and blindfold for game

Instructional Activities	Teaching Hints

Introductory Activity – Countdown

Standing with arms stretched overhead, students begin a countdown (10, 9, 8, 7, etc.) and gradually lower themselves into a crouched position with each count. On the words "blast off," they jump upwards, cheer, and run in different directions.

Try different variations such as:
1. Different locomotor movements.
2. Change speed of counting-slow, fast.
3. Point to a student who says, "Blast Off!"

Fitness Development Activity – Parachute Fitness

1. Jog while holding the chute in the left hand. (music)
2. Shake the chute. (no music)
3. Slide while holding the chute with both hands. (music)
4. Sit and perform curl-ups. (no music)
5. Skip. (music)
6. Freeze, face the center, and stretch the chute tightly. Repeat five to six times. (no music)
7. Run in place while holding the chute taut at different levels. (music)
8. Sit with legs under the chute. Do a seat walk toward the center. Return to the perimeter. Repeat four to six times. (no music)
9. Place the chute on the ground. Jog away from the chute and return on signal. Repeat. (music)
10. Move into push-up position holding the chute with one hand. Shake the chute. (no music)
11. Shake the chute and jump in place. (music)
12. Lie on back with feet under the chute. Shake the chute with the feet. (no music)
13. Hop to the center of the chute and return. Repeat. (music)
14. Sit with feet under the chute. Stretch by touching the toes with the chute. Relax with other stretches while sitting. (no music)

Tape alternating segments (20-25 seconds in length) of silence and music to signal duration of exercise. Music segments indicate aerobic activity with the parachute while intervals of silence announce using the chute to enhance flexibility and strength development.

Space youngsters evenly around the chute.

Use different hand grips (palms up, down, mixed).

All movements should be done under control. Some of the faster and stronger students will have to moderate their performance.

Lesson Focus -- Rhythmic Movement (4)

Make dances easy for students to learn by implementing some of the following techniques:
1. Teach the dances without using partners.
2. Allow youngsters to move in any direction without left-right orientation.
3. Use scattered formation instead of circles.
4. Emphasize strong movements such as clapping and stamping to increase involvement.
5. Play the music at a slower speed when first learning the dance.

Teach a variety of dances rather than one or two in depth in case some students find it difficult to master a specific dance.
Records can be ordered from Wagon Wheel Records, 17191 Corbina Lane #203, Huntington Beach, CA (714) 846-8169.

The Muffin Man (American)

Record: LS E-1
Formation: Single circle, facing center, hands at sides. One child, the Muffin Man, stands in front of another child.
Directions:
Verse 1: The children stand still and clap their hands lightly, with the exception of the Muffin Man and his partner. These two join hands and jump lightly in place while keeping time to the music. On the first beat of each measure, a normal jump is taken, followed by a bounce in place (rebound) on the second beat.
Verse 2: The Muffin Man and his partner then skip around the inside of the circle individually and, near the end of the verse, each stands in front of a child, their new partner.
Verse 1 is then repeated, with two sets of partners doing the jumping. During the repetition of verse 2, four children skip around the inside of the circle and choose partners. This procedure continues until all children have been chosen.

Seven Jumps (Danish)

Records: LS E-8; MAV 1043; RM 2
Formation: Single circle, hands joined
Directions:
There are seven jumps to the dance. Each jump is preceded by the following action.

Measures	Action
1--8	The circle moves to the right with seven step-hops, one to each measure. On the eighth measure, all jump high in the air and reverse direction. (Step-hop, 2-hop, 3-hop, . . . 7-hop, change direction)
9--16	Circle to the left with seven step-hops. Stop on measure 16 and face the center. (Step-hop, 2-hop, 3-hop, . . . 7-hop, face center)
17	All drop hands, place their hands on hips, and lift the right knee upward with the toes pointed downward. (Knee up)
18	All stamp the right foot to the ground on the signal note, then join hands on the next note. (Stamp)
1--18	Repeat measures 1--18, but do not join hands.
19	Lift the left knee, stamp, and join hands.
1--19	Repeat measures 1--19, but do not join hands.
20	Put the right toe backward and kneel on the right knee. Stand and join hands.
1--20	Repeat measures 1--20; do not join hands.
21	Kneel on the left knee. Stand and join hands.
1--21	Repeat measures 1--21; do not join hands.
22	Put the right elbow to the floor with the cheek on the fist. Stand and join hands.
1--22	Repeat measures 1--22; do not join hands.
23	Put the left elbow to the floor with the cheek on the fist. Stand and join hands.
1--23	Repeat measures 1--23; do not join hands.
24	Put the forehead on the floor. Stand and join hands.
1--16	Repeat measures 1--16.

To increase motivation, the dance can be done with a parachute. The dancers hold the parachute taut with one hand during the step-hops. The chute is kept taut with both hands for all jumps except the last, during which the forehead touches the chute on the floor.

Pease Porridge Hot (English)

Record: LS E-8
Formation: Double circle, partners facing
Directions:
The dance is in two parts. The first is a pat-a-cake rhythm done while the children sing the verse. During the second part, partners dance in a circular movement.

Part I Action
Line 1: Slap the hands to the thighs, clap the hands together, clap the hands to partner's hands. (Thighs, together, partner)
Line 2: Repeat the action of line 1.
Line 3: Slap the hands to the thighs, clap the hands together, clap the right hand against partner's right, clap one's own hands together. (Thighs, together, right, together)
Line 4: Clap the left hand to partner's left, clap one's own hands together, clap both hands against partner's hands. (Left, together, both)
Lines 5--8: Repeat lines 1--4.

Part II Action
Join both hands with partner and run around in a small circle (an elbow swing can be used), turning counterclockwise for the first four lines and ending with the word "old!" (Run)
Reverse direction and run clockwise for the remainder of the verse. (Change direction)
Move one step to the left for a new partner. (New partner)

Yankee Doodle (American)

Records: Windsor 7S1; LS E-10
Formation: Scattered or open circle facing counterclockwise
Directions:

Measures	Action
1--4	All gallop 8 steps (Gallop, 2, . . . 8)
5--8	All stop, face center, point to cap and bow on word "macaroni." (Stop, point, bow)
9—12	All join hands and take six slides to the right and stamp feet two times on word "dandy." (Slide, 2, 3, . . . 6; Stamp, stamp)
13--16	All slide six times to the left and clap hands two times on the word "candy." (Slide, 2, 3, . . . 6; Clap clap)

Change the locomotor movements to fit the age and interest of the group. Have the class create new movement patterns.

Eins Zwei Drei (German)

Record: HLP-4026

Formation: Single circle of couples (partner B to partner A's right) facing the center and numbered alternately couple 1, 2, 1, 2

Directions:

Explain that "Eins, Zwei, Drei" means "one, two, three" in German.

Measures	Part I Action
1—2	Couples 1 take three steps toward the center of the circle as they clap their hands by brushing them vertically like cymbals. (Forward, 2, 3, pause)
3--4	Couples 1 repeat measures 1--2, walking backward to place. (Back, 2, 3, pause)
5—8	Couples 1 face, join both hands, and take four slides toward the center of the circle and four slides back to place. Partner A starts with the left foot, partner B with the right. (Slide, 2, 3, 4)
9--16	Couples 2 repeat measures 1--8.

Measures	Part II Action
17	Partner A turns and touches the right heel sideward while shaking the right index finger at partner. Partner B does the same with the left heel and left index finger. (Scold, 2, 3)
18	Repeat measure 17 with the corner, reversing footwork and hands. (Scold, 2, 3)
19--20	Repeat measures 17 and 18.
21--24	All join hands and circle left with eight slides. (Slide, 2, 3, . . . 8)
25--32	Repeat measures 17--24, reversing the direction of the slides. (Slide, 2, 3, . . . 8)

Game Activity

Circle Stoop

Supplies: Music or tom-tom

Skills: Moving to rhythm

Children are in a single circle, facing counterclockwise. A march or similar music, or a tom-tom beat, can be used. The children march with good posture until the music stops. As soon as a child no longer hears the music or the tom-tom beat, he stoops and touches both hands to the ground without losing his balance. The last child to touch both hands to the ground and those children who lost balance pay a penalty by going into the mush pot (the center of the circle) and waiting out the next round of the game. The children must march in good posture, and anyone stooping, even partially, before the music stops should be penalized. The duration of the music should be varied.

Variations:

1. Using suitable music, have children employ different locomotor movements, such as skipping, hopping, or galloping.

2. Vary the stooping position. Instead of stooping, use positions such as the Push-Up, Crab, or Lame Dog, or balancing on one foot or touching with one hand and one foot. Such variations add to the interest and fun.

Blindfolded Duck

Supplies: A wand, broomstick, cane, or yardstick

Skills: Fundamental locomotor movements

One child, designated the duck (Daisy if a girl, Donald if a boy), stands blindfolded in the center of a circle and holds a wand or similar article. She taps on the floor and tells children to hop (or perform some other locomotor movement). Children in the circle act accordingly, all moving in the same direction. Daisy then taps the wand twice on the floor, which signals all children to stop. Daisy moves forward with her wand, still blindfolded, to find a child in the circle. She asks, "Who are you?" The child responds, "Quack, quack." Daisy tries to identify this person. If the guess is correct, the identified child becomes the new duck. If the guess is wrong, Daisy must take another turn. After two unsuccessful turns, another child is chosen to be the duck.

Lesson Plans for Grades K-2 - Week 35
Movement Skills and Concepts (10)
Twisting, Turning, Stretching and Relaxing Movements

Objectives:
To independently select an active introductory activity
To relax muscle groups
To recognize and perform twisting and turning movements

Equipment Required:
Teacher's choice of equipment for
introductory activity and manipulative
skills in the lesson focus

Instructional Activities	Teaching Hints

Introductory Activity – Creative and Exploratory Opportunities

Put out enough equipment for all children to have a piece. Allow them to explore and create activities while moving. Another alternative is to have students work with a piece of equipment with a partner or small group.

Ask students to move and be active without being told what to do. Encourage independent thinking.

Fitness Development Activity -- Animal Movements and Fitness Challenges

1. Puppy Dog Walk --30 seconds.
2. Freeze; perform stretching activities.
3. Measuring Worm Walk—30 seconds
4. Freeze; perform abdominal development challenges.
5. Seal Crawl --30 seconds.
6. Freeze; perform push-up position challenges.
7. Elephant Walk --30 seconds.
8. Injured Coyote Walk--30 seconds.
9. Freeze; perform abdominal challenges.
10. Crab Walk—30 seconds.
11. Rabbit Jump

Tape alternating segments (30 seconds in length) of silence and music to signal duration of exercise. Music segments indicate performing animal movements while intervals of silence announce doing the fitness challenges.

A variation is to place animal movement signs throughout the area and instruct students to move from sign to sign performing the appropriate animal movement each time they reach a new sign.

Lesson Focus Movement Skills and Concepts (10)

Fundamental Skill: Twisting
1. Glue your feet to the floor. Can you twist your body to the right and to the left? Can you twist slowly, quickly? Can you bend and twist at the same time? How far can you twist your hands back and forth?
2. Twist two parts of the body at the same time. Try three. More?
3. Can you twist one part of the body in one direction and another in a different direction?
4. Is it possible to twist the upper half of your body without twisting the lower part? How about the reverse?
5. Seated on the floor, what parts of the body can you twist?
6. Can you twist one part of the body around another? Why or why not?
7. Balance on one foot and twist your body. Can you bend and twist in this position?
8. Show different shapes that can be made using twisted body parts.

Select a few activities from each of the categories so students receive a variety of skills to practice. When possible, integrate the manipulative skill activities with fundamental skill activities. A common error is to teach all the activities from one category. The reason for multiple groups of activities is to provide variety and enhance motivation.

Teach youngsters the difference between a twist and turn. Twisting is rotating a selected body part around it own long axis. Twisting involves movement around the body part itself while turning focuses on the space in which the body turns. Turning here involves movement of the entire body.

Fundamental Skill: Turning
1. Turn your body left and right with quarter and half turns. Turn clockwise and counterclockwise.
2. Post compass directions on the walls--north, south, east, and west. Have children face the correct direction on call. Introduce some in-between directions--northwest, southeast, etc.
3. Can you stand on one foot and turn around slowly, quickly, with a series of small hops?
4. Show me how you can cross your legs with a turn and then sit down. Can you get up without moving your feet too much.

Emphasize maintaining balance while performing turning activities.

5. When you hear the signal, turn completely around one. Next time turn the other way. Now try with two full turns; three.

Perform twisting and turning movements in both directions. Also, try the movements in sitting or on tummy.

6. Lie on your tummy and turn yourself around in an arc. Try seated position.

Fundamental Skill: Rocking

1. How many different ways can your rock? Which part of the body is used to rock the highest?

Make rocking a smooth and steady rhythm. It should be a controlled movement.

2. Select a part of the body and show me how you ca rock smoothly and slowly. How about quickly and smoothly?
3. Can you rock like a rocking chair?
4. Lie on your back and rock. Point both hands and feet toward the ceiling and rock on the back.

Rocking is usually best done when the body surface is rounded. Discuss how the body can be rounded to make rocking easier.

5. Lie on your tummy and rock. Rock as high as you can. Can you hold your ankles and make giant rocks?
6. Can you rock in a standing position? Try forward, sideways and diagonal rocking directions.
7. Select a position where you can rock and twist at the same time.
8. Who can lie on his or her back, with knees up and rock side to side?

Manipulative Skill: Student's Choice

Select one or more manipulative activities that need additional developing with respect to the children's needs and progress. During the week's work, a different activity might be scheduled each individual day.

Since equipment was placed out for the introductory activity, use it for the manipulative skill.

Movement Concept: Stretching and Curling

1. While on your feet, show us a stretched position. A curled position.
2. Go very slowly from your stretched position to the curled one you select. Go rapidly.

Stretching and curling are somewhat opposite movements.

3. Keeping one foot in place (on a spot), show how far you can stretch in different directions.

Encourage stretching through the full range of movement. The stretch is done slowly and smoothly.

4. Show us a straight (regular) curled position. A twisted curled position. A tight curled position.
5. Select three different curled positions. On signal, go from one to the other rapidly. Repeat with stretch positions.

Encourage holding the stretch for 6-10 seconds.

6. Explore and show the different ways that the body can support itself in curled positions.

Movement Concept: Tension and Relaxation

1. Make yourself as tense as possible. Now relax.
2. Take a deep breath, hold it tight. Expel the air and relax.
3. Reach as high as you can tensed, slowly relax and droop to the floor.
4. Show how you can tense different parts of the body.

Relaxation activities are an excellent way to finish the lesson. Help youngsters learn to recognize when a limb and muscles are relaxed.

5. Tense one part of the body and relax another. Shift the tenseness to the relaxes part and vice-versa.
6. Press your fingers hard against your tensed abdominal muscles. Take your fists and best lightly against the tensed position. Relax. Repeat.

Relaxing is facilitated by a quiet atmosphere. Soft voices encourage students to "wind down."

7. Move forward, stop suddenly in a tensed position. Relax. Repeat.

Game Activity

Midnight
   Supplies: None
   Skills: Running, dodging
   A safety line is established about 40 ft from a den in which one player, the fox, is standing. The others stand behind the safety line and move forward slowly, asking, "Please, Mr. Fox, what time is it?" The fox answers in various fashions, such as "Bedtime," "Pretty late," "Three-thirty." The fox continues to draw the players toward him. At some point, he answers the question by saying "Midnight," and then chases the others back to the safety line. Any player who is caught joins the fox in the den and helps to catch others. No player in the den may leave, however, until the fox calls out "Midnight."

Twins (Triplets)

     Supplies: None

     Skills: Body management

     Youngsters find a space in the area. Each youngster has a partner (twin). The teacher gives commands such as "Take three hops and two leaps" or "Walk backward four steps and three skips." When the pairs are separated, the teacher says, "Find your twin!" Players find their twin and stand frozen back to back. The goal is to not be the last pair to find each other and assume the frozen position.

     Students need to move away from each other during the movements. One alternative is to find a new twin each time. Another variation is to separate twins in opposite ends of the playing area.

Variation: The game becomes more challenging when played in groups of three (triplets). When using this variation, new partners should be selected each time.

Lesson Plans for Grades K-2 - Week 36
Partner Manipulative Activities Using Playground Balls

Objectives:
To catch a passed ball from a partner
To pass a ball to a partner (both chest and bounce pass)
To dribble a ball

Equipment Required:
One 8½" playground ball for each pair of students
Bowling pins for targets (optional)

Instructional Activities	Teaching Hints

Introductory Activity – Airplanes

Children pretend to be airplanes. They take off, zoom with arms out, swoop, turn, and glide. On signal, they drop to the floor in prone position. To takeoff again, they must "restart" their engines by doing a couple of push-up challenges while making a "vroom, vroom" engine sound.

Encourage creativity by naming different types of airplanes and helicopters.

Use different locomotor movements.

Fitness Development Activity --Astronaut Drills

1. Walk.
2. Walk on tiptoes while reaching for the sky.
3. Walk with giant strides.
4. Freeze; perform various stretches.
5. Do a Puppy Dog Walk.
6. Jump like a pogo stick.
7. Freeze; perform Push-up challenges.
8. Walk and swing arms like a helicopter.
9. Trot lightly and silently.
10. Slide like and athlete.
11. Freeze; perform Curl-up challenges.
12. Crab Walk.
13. Skip
14. Freeze; perform trunk development challenges.
15. Walk and cool down.

Tape alternating segments of silence and music to signal duration of exercise. Music segments (30 seconds in duration) indicate locomotor activities while intervals of silence (30 seconds) announce freezing and performing flexibility and strength development activities.

See text, p. 163-167 for descriptions of challenges.

Lesson Focus -- Manipulative Activities with a Partner Using Playground Balls

1. Rolling a ball back and forth to a partner.
   a. Practice different deliveries, i.e., two-handed, right and left.
   b. Roll at targets such as bowling pins or through the legs of a partner.
2. Dribbling and Passing Skills.
   a. One player guards and the other dribbles. Change on signal. Practice with both hands.
   b. Practice passing back and forth to a partner. Use the chest pass.
   c. Pass back and forth using the bounce pass.
   d. Combine passing and dribbling. Dribble the ball 3 times and pass to partner.
3. Rolling and Passing from different positions.
   a. Try rolling and passing skills from different positions, i.e., kneeling, sitting.
4. Passing and Moving
   a. One child remains in place and passes to the other child, who is moving. The moving child can trace different patterns, such as back and forth between two spots or in a circle around the stationary child.
   b. Practice different kinds of throws and passes as both children move in different patterns.
   c. Practice foot skills of dribbling and passing.
   d. Partners hold the ball between their bodies without using the hands or arms. Experiment with different ways to move together.
   d. Carrying a ball, run in different directions while partner follows. On signal, toss the ball upward so that the child following can catch it. Now change places and repeat the activity.
5. Try following activity; one partner leads a ball activity and the other follows.
6. Allow time for students to explore and create.

Encourage proper skill performance by using instructional cues such as:
"Keep your eyes on the ball."
"Catch the ball with the pads of the fingers and thumb."
"Use opposition when passing the ball."

When catching, soft receipt of the ball is achieved by "giving" with the hands and arms. The hands should reach out somewhat to receive the ball and then cushion the impact by bringing the ball toward the body.

To catch a throw above the waist, the hands should be positioned so that the thumbs are together. To receive a throw below the waist, the little fingers should be kept toward each other and the thumbs kept out.

In throwing to a partner, unless otherwise specified, the throw should reach the partner at about chest height. At times, different target points should be specified---high, low, right, left.

Game Activity

Stork Tag

Supplies: None

Skills: Fundamental locomotor movements, dodging

Children are scattered about the area. One child is it and chases the others, trying to tag one of them. When a tag is made, she says, "You're it." The new it chases other children. Children are safe when they move into the stork position which is assumed by balancing on one foot with the eyes closed. The sole of the foot must be placed alongside the knee to complete the stork position. The stork position can be held until the lifted foot touches the floor; students are then eligible to be tagged.

Flowers and Wind

Supplies: None

Skill: Running

Two parallel lines long enough to accommodate the children are drawn about 30 ft apart. Children are divided into two groups. One is the wind and the other the flowers. Each of the teams takes a position on one of the lines and faces the other team. The flowers secretly select the name of a common flower. When ready, they walk over to the other line and stand about 3 ft away from the wind. The players on the wind team begin to call out flower names--trying to guess the flower chosen. When the flower has been guessed, the flowers run to their goal line, chased by the players of the other team. Any player caught must join the other side. The roles are reversed and the game is repeated. If one side has trouble guessing, a clue can be given to the color or size of the flower or the first letter of its name.